FROM ELizabeth Christmas 1986.
MRS. M. PLUMMER,
184, OLD BEDFORD ROAD,
LUTON,
BEDFORDSHIRE.

ROYAL CHRISTMAS BOOK

ROYAL CHRISTMAS BOOK

Michèle Brown

WINDWARD

Royal Christmas Book

Created by Antler Books Ltd, 11 Rathbone Place, London W1P 1DE

Produced by Tom Williams

Picture Research by Susan Bilton

Original concept by Jane Davan Wetton

©Antler Books Ltd 1985

First Published by Windward an imprint
owned by W H Smith & Son Ltd
Registered No 237811 England
Trading as W H S Distributors St John's House, East Street,
Leicester LE1 6NE

ISBN 0 7112 0427 6

Typesetting by BWS Graphics, London EC1
Film and separations by BBE Colour Ltd, Chelmsford,
Essex
Printed by Purnell & Sons (Book Production) Ltd

Copyright reserved. Pictures on the following pages are
reproduced by gracious permission of Her Majesty The
Queen: 6/7, 12/13, 20/21, 46/47, 52/53, 54/55, 58/59,
62/63, 66/67, 68/69, 70/71, 82/83, 86/87, 90/91, 92/93,
94/95, 112/113, 114/115, 126/127

Alpha, 28/29, 84/85, 108/109, 118/119
Associated Newspapers, 96/97
BBC, 78/79
British Museum, 14/15, 16/17, 80/81, 88/89
Lionel Cherruault, 98/99, 110/111
Country Life, 60/61
Daily Telegraph, 24/25
Eastern Daily Press, 100/101
Mary Evans Picture Library, frontispiece
Fox Photos, 32/33
Michael Gell, 36/37, 40/41
Tim Graham, 106/107
Anwar Hussein, 26/27, 30/31, 64/65, 74/75
David Levinson/Colorific, 122/123
Mansell Collection, 34/35
National Geographic Society (James L. Stanfield), cover and 38/39
Photo Source, 56/57, 104/105, 116/117
Popperfoto, 102/103, 120/121, 124/125
Royal College of Music, 8/9
Royal Pavilion Brighton, 44/45
John Shelley, 22/23, 50/51
Snowdon, 42/43
Victoria and Albert Museum; 10/11, 18/19

Plan of Windsor Castle on page 48/49 produced by MJL
Cartographics

Introduction

The Queen and her family provide a focus for the unity of our country, which is made up of many different elements, and for the unity of the Commonwealth, which is made up of many different countries. They do this in two ways; in the ceremonial which reminds us of our history and traditions and on an informal level by being a family in whose daily life, its good times and bad times, everyone can find something with which they can identify.

Christmas is probably the most important family occasion of the year; it is a time when people seek to bury their differences and emphasise the positive and optimistic side of life. The way in which the Royal Family spends its Christmas may be on a somewhat grander scale than the rest of us (forty people at lunch and a Christmas tree some twenty foot tall), but by and large the Queen and millions of her people share the same experience. It is on the level of family life — the marriages, holidays, christenings and annual festivities and festivals — that most of us relate best to the phenomenon of monarchy.

This book is crammed with insights about the way our present Royal Family spend their Christmas and how the Queen's ancestors helped create the way we celebrate Christmas today. When William the Conqueror was King, nine hundred years ago, the court spent Christmas at Gloucester; now the Queen goes to another of his castles, Windsor. But some small details remain surprisingly the same. In the middle ages boar's head and roast peacock dressed in its own feathers were the most prized Christmas dishes. In 1935 George V ate roast peacock for his Christmas lunch and boar's head is still the pièce de résistance on the royal sideboard at Windsor. Some aspects of life may change alarmingly fast but two traditions, Christmas and the Royal Family, remain reassuringly the same.

The Royal Family and our Christmas tradition

The traditional Christmas enjoyed in Britain today is based to a great extent on the German fashion of celebrating Christmas, and dates back at least two hundred years. From the beginning of the eighteenth century, when the Hanoverian Kings from Germany succeeded the Stuarts, the German way of celebrating Christmas began to seep into the British way of life.

When Prince Albert of Saxe Coburg married Queen Victoria in 1840 he brought with him a love and respect for his country's traditions which his wife eagerly adopted. Both of them believed in the importance of a happy and united family life and loved the annual feasts and festivals which helped to strenghten it. For them, as for most people, Christmas was the most important family season, and the way in which Victoria and her family kept Christmas was copied by everyone who looked to them to set the pattern for a happy domestic life. So when Prince Albert set up a Christmas tree at Windsor Castle for the first Christmas of his eldest child, the Princess Royal, it was not long before

Christmas trees, used infrequently till then, became widely fashionable in homes throughout the country.

Occasionally artists or photographers were allowed to depict the royal Christmas trees so we have a good impression of how they looked, their chief feature being the hundreds of tiny wax candles which illuminated them during the present-giving on Christmas Day and again on New Year's Day, and on Twelfth Night, before the trees were dismantled.

The royal couple also 'invented' their own tradition of displaying their gifts on separate tables set out around the room, with a tree and table specially for the children. This tradition is continued at Windsor to the present day with a tree from the Sandringham estate and long tables of presents set up in the Red Drawing Room.

Nearly one hundred and fifty years later Elizabeth II and her people continue to celebrate Christmas with all the customs and traditions popularised by her great-great-grandfather.

J. Roberts,
Watercolour of
Queen Victoria's
Christmas Trees,
1850

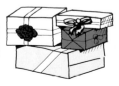

THE
COLLECTED COMPOSITIONS
OF
HIS ROYAL HIGHNESS
THE PRINCE CONSORT.

THE
COLLECTED COMPOSITIONS
OF
His Royal Highness.
THE PRINCE CONSORT.

Edited by
W. G. CUSINS.

PRICE ONE GUINEA.

LONDON:
METZLER & C?, 37, GREAT MARLBOROUGH STREET, W.

CHRISTMAS

HYMN.

——

ALBERT.

Carols and Christmas music

Carols have been a part of the Christmas season for Kings and commoners ever since the middle ages. Music always played a prominent part in Court life, not only as straightforward entertainment but as part of the ceremonial which bolstered up the monarch's prestige. Music was important for impressing visiting foreign dignitaries, for making ceremonies like the Coronation more impressive and for increasing morale at tournaments and in battle. Several British monarchs have been talented musicians, and none more so than Henry VIII, although it is doubtful that he really did write the famous song 'Greensleeves'. In the sixteenth century England was famous for its good music and Henry was greatly respected by his fellow musicians. He is known to have written at least one song for the Christmas season — 'Green groweth the holly'. The chorus of this runs:

> Green grow'th the holly, So doth the ivy,
> Though winter blast blow never so high;
> Green grow'th the holly.

However, not surprisingly for a man who had six wives, the King turns the Christmas song into a love song with the words:

> As the holly grow'th green
> And never changeth hew,
> So I am, ever hath been
> Unto my lady true.

Prince Albert, who influenced so much of the way we celebrate Christmas, was also a talented amateur musician, and at Christmas he naturally favoured the Christmas hymns from his German homeland. He was friendly with many musicians, Mendelssohn in particular. Music flourished at Buckingham Palace and Windsor under the Prince's enthusiastic direction, and many composers, including Mendelssohn, came to England to perform before the Queen. Prince Albert himself was capable of composing songs which, though not technically perfect, were successful in appealing to people's emotions. He left a large body of work, some of which was collected and published under the editorship of the Master of the Queen's Music. This setting of 'Hark the Herald Angels Sing' appears in that collection.

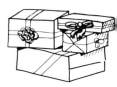

The first Christmas cards

The Christmas card is one of the major features of Christmas which can be dated back quite specifically to the reign of Queen Victoria. Unlike so much else, which bore the imprint of the Prince Consort's enthusiasm for the German-style of Christmas, the first commercial, printed Christmas card was quite definitely an English invention. It was drawn in 1843 by the artist John Calcott Horsley at the suggestion of his friend Henry Cole, an eminent Victorian reformer and philanthropist, whose championing of the penny post did much to make sending the cards simpler and cheaper.

Of course the habit of exchanging greetings at Christmas goes back long before the Christmas card. After the invention of printing in the fifteenth century it became fashionable for the rich to give each other engravings with a seasonal theme. Later, tradesmen took to printing Christmas verses and leaving them with their customers in the hope of being rewarded with a large Christmas tip. By the beginning of the nineteenth century 'Christmas Pieces' were popular. These were decorated sheets of paper with a space left for writing your own particular greeting. They were much used by schoolchildren as a means of proving to their parents how well their writing was coming along.

As well as the convenience of the penny post one of the reasons why Christmas cards did not die out like so many earlier fashions was the development of an early form of colour printing. This meant that the cards were much more bright and cheerful than anything before. Modern Christmas cards are sometimes criticised for becoming too 'commercial' but in fact the earliest cards, like the one shown here, rarely had any religious theme. Horsley's card depicted scenes from a family Christmas. In later years this theme was joined by a wide variety of subjects — robins, mistletoe, family pets, holly, sledges, Christmas food, beautiful women, the seasons, Christmas trees, Christmas parties, flowers, Columbine and Harlequin, snow scenes, attractive children, fashionable Japanese designs — the varieties were endless.

A·MERRY·CHRISTMAS·AND·A·HAPPY·NEW·YEAR.

V.A.M.

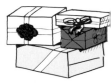

The new Year

for Mama & Papa

from

Vicky

Home-made Victorian cards

This delightful Christmas/New Year card was drawn for Queen Victoria and the Prince Consort by their eldest daughter Princess Vicky, the Princess Royal. The royal children were all taught to draw and paint. The Queen herself was a prolific artist, especially fond of portraying her family and her houses, so naturally she encouraged her nine children to become proficient in a pastime which gave her so much pleasure.

Princess Vicky was just thirteen years old when she made this card. She was always her father's favourite child, he loved her quick intelligence and the fact that she shared so many of his interests. So the Prince, as well as Queen Victoria, felt bereft when she was married at the age of seventeen, even though it was a love match with the Crown Prince of the greatest German state, Prussia, and so strengthened the links between Britain and Germany. Inevitably it was the very first Christmas, when the Queen and her husband were not surrounded by all their children, which brought home to them how much they missed their beloved elder daughter.

This is touchingly clear from the thank you letter written by the Queen to Vicky.

Windsor Castle, Christmas day 1858
How can I sufficiently thank you for your dear gifts? That beautiful quilt – your own dear work – which shall go about with me everywhere, and the lovely bracelet from you both which is on my arm – so like, so pretty, so nicely set and gives me immense pleasure. Dearest child, I missed your dear, warm, affectionate hearty greeting – your busy anxious endeavours to help and please us all! No-one showed this more than you, my dearest child! – You are constantly in our thoughts – but your dear letter and your gifts – the kind and touching way in which you thought of us all (for which God bless your warm, loving heart) brought you very near to us, and our spirits joined at least.'

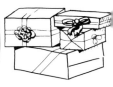

Novelty cards and family mementoes

As Christmas cards became increasingly popular manufacturers vied with each other to produce the most interesting novelty cards. This is a purse card, a type which became very fashionable towards the end of the nineteenth century. The purse, and its almost equally ornate envelope, were delicately scented and when it was opened a cent coin was found inside. This particular purse card was sent to seven-year-old Princess May (later Queen Mary) by her mother Princess Mary Adelaide, for Christmas 1874.

Queen Mary was an avid collector all her life. As well as antiques and works of art she collected family mementoes and made scrap books of them. Queen Mary's collection of Christmas cards is particularly interesting because it provides us with a fascinating insight into the day to day relationships of the Royal Family. Cards to Queen Mary's husband (later George V) from Queen Victoria are signed 'To darling Georgie from his loving grandmamma VRE.' Six-year-old Prince Henry (later the Duke of Gloucester) gave Queen Mary a card, of a dish of fruit, which he had coloured with crayons and outlined in back-stitch. It was signed 'For dear Mama from Harry.' For Christmas 1904 his brother, nine-year-old Prince Albert (the future George VI), sent his father a picture postcard of Windsor Castle which he had personalised by crayoning it in and adding a flag, with the name 'Bertie', to the top of the famous Round Tower.

Not all the cards in the Queen Mary Collection are family cards. One unusual example, given to the Prince of Wales in 1929 is a single grain of rice, inscribed 'To His Royal Highness The Prince of Wales, Sincere Christmas Greetings From the Joseph G. Gillott Pen Co., London, England. Season 1929.' Queen Mary also treasured the cards sent to her by ordinary men and women, especially cards sent to her by servicemen during the Second World War. These make up many of the albums in her collection which is now kept in the British Museum.

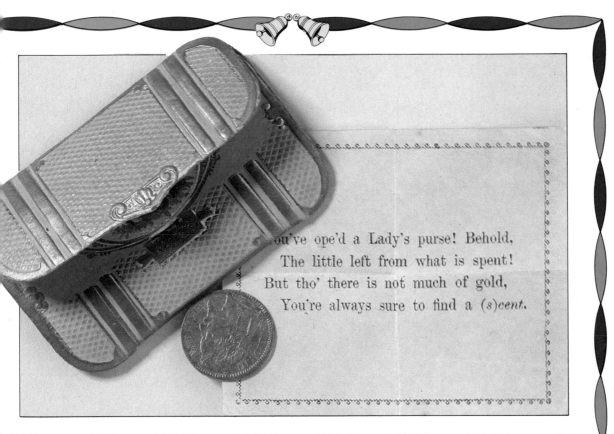

You've ope'd a Lady's purse! Behold,
The little left from what is spent!
But tho' there is not much of gold,
You're always sure to find a *(s)cent*.

CHRISTMAS·JOY·BELLS
ARE·RINGING·FOR·YOU

To Grannie

From Lilibet

19³³

Princess Elizabeth's Christmas

As she grew older, Queen Mary appeared formidable and in some ways rather intimidating, yet to her grandchildren she was simply 'Grannie'. This home-made card was given to Queen Mary by Princess Elizabeth in 1933, when the Princess was seven years old. Its charm for us is that it is so like the home-made cards which all children are encouraged to make at school for their families. The bells, the horseshoes and the lettering are all done in gold and the inscription is written in pencil. Lilibet was Princess Elizabeth's baby name which was used by the entire family.

Home-made cards were just one way in which the Duke and Duchess of York (later George VI and Queen Elizabeth) tried to keep their daughters from becoming spoilt. They were not given expensive jewellery and presents but learned to appreciate small treasures, like the fudge which the nurserymaid used to make and the necklaces and bracelets they had strung themselves from glass beads.

Like other children they wrote letters to Father Christmas about the presents they wanted and made shopping lists of what to buy for family and friends. Some of this shopping was done in Harrods but quite a lot came from Woolworth's, where it was possible to buy things with small amounts of pocket money. A list of presents requiring thank you letters, which Princess Elizabeth made as a reminder for Princess Margaret, gives a good idea of the type of gifts which were given to children in the Royal Family. From her mother Princess Margaret had received a see-saw and a doll with dresses, from her father an umbrella and from Grannie a calendar. Their parents also filled a stocking with small trinkets. Afterwards Princess Elizabeth liked to tidy away the pieces of wrapping paper, silver paper and ribbon, many of which were recycled or used for home-made cards like the ones she gave to her Grannie, Queen Mary.

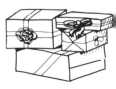

Our very own cards

The three previous Christmas cards are all private ones, sent and received by members of the Royal Family. Here the Royal Family is itself the subject of a Christmas card. An unexpected image of Princess Elizabeth and the Duke of Edinburgh, it depicts them square dancing at the Rideau Hall in Ottawa in October 1951. The card is taken from a painting by H. Hassell. It was commissioned by the famous Canadian brewing company, Carling, to commemorate the Queen's 1957 visit to Canada, and used as a Christmas card in 1958.

Elizabeth II is not only Queen of the United Kingdom but also of nine other countries, including Canada. She visits Canada frequently and during their 1951 tour she and the Duke of Edinburgh watched and joined in many typical Canadian activities, including the Calgary rodeo. A famous newspaper picture from that tour showed the Princess and her husband thoroughly enjoying themselves during a boisterous square dance and the Hassell painting was based on that photograph. In the Queen Mary Collection there is a much earlier Canadian Christmas card — a photograph of a typical Canadian train! It was sent to Queen Mary from Ottawa by her cousin the Duchess of Connaught.

Pictures of the Royal Family have often been used as Christmas cards, not least by the family themselves. They love family photographs, so many of their private cards are family groups. Some of the earliest are informal snapshots which give a good impression of what life was like for the off-duty Royal Family. Many of the cards include foreign relatives, all with a marked family resemblance; and what comes across strongly is a sense of family unity.

As well as personal cards the Queen sends out hundreds of official cards every year, often to people who are recommended to her by close members of her staff. These are nearly always formal family portrait photographs with a simple signature inside. They are greatly prized by those who receive them and the few which become available are much sought after by collectors.

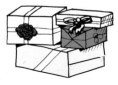

Watercolour attributed to Egon Lundgren, Gillies' Ball, Balmoral, 1859.

Staff Christmas parties

The Royal Family choose the Christmas season to thank the hundreds of staff who serve them, for their loyalty and hard work throughout the year. This means Christmas presents for everyone and usually at least one staff Christmas party. The Queen Mother's parties at Clarence House are always particularly enjoyable but of course most of the entertaining is done by the Queen, who employs hundreds of people at Buckingham Palace alone.

The Christmas party for staff at the Queen's residences alternates on a system of two years at Buckingham Palace, then two years at Windsor. Because of the huge numbers involved most people are invited every other year. Even so the party is an impressive occasion with at least seven hundred guests. Catering is done by Lyons, the people who cater for thousands of garden party guests in the summer. This enables the kitchen and serving staff to enjoy a genuine night off. The Queen and her family spend some time at the party, mingling informally and chatting.

For the New Year the family moves to Sandringham, which is much smaller and more homely than Windsor or Buckingham Palace, and on New Year's Day the Queen takes the opportunity to give individual presents to each member of the Sandringham staff.

The Royal Family are only at Balmoral, the Queen's Scottish residence, in the summer, When Queen Victoria and Prince Albert stayed at Balmoral one of the highlights of their visit was the staff party, the Gillies' Ball, which took place shortly before the Queen returned to London in September. For many years after Albert's death this event was organised by the Queen's much-loved Scottish servant John Brown. Despite the often rowdy and uninhibited nature of the affair the Queen loved it and rarely missed it. The tradition continues in the twentieth century. There are now two Gillies' Balls at Balmoral every summer which are the equivalent to the Christmas parties in England. The painting shown here is of the Gillies' Ball in 1859, and depicts the Royal Family watching a traditional Scottish dance.

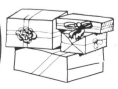

Count-down to Christmas

As the Queen's political role has declined her importance as a figurehead has increased. She is now expected to be much more accessible than any monarch before her and to be available for a wide variety of engagements — formal and informal. To help meet the infinite demands on her time the Queen relies heavily on the other members of her family who deputise for her and bring the mystique of Royalty to a wider audience than would be possible if the Queen did everything herself. So when Lady Diana Spencer became engaged to the Prince of Wales one of the questions posed most often by the press was 'How will she cope with her public duties?' Prince Charles had already proved an able and popular substitute for his mother. His success is in part due to the incalculable advantage of having been brought up to cope with the unusual way of life he leads. Diana Spencer was used to living the life of an unrestricted teenager. Moreover she was clearly rather shy and did not appear confident in public.

It is hard now, with photographs of the attractive, self-assured Princess appearing in the newspaper every day, to remember that her ability was ever in question. This success is partly because Diana was introduced gradually to what was expected of her. She was accompanied by Prince Charles on all her initial public engagements, and made her first public speech while touring Wales with him shortly after their wedding. It was not until Christmas of the same year that she made her first solo public appearance when she switched on the Regent Street lights. These lights were introduced in 1954 to brighten up Christmas in the West End after years of war and rationing. Prince Charles performed the ceremony on his thirtieth birthday in 1978 and a member of the Royal Family has done so on most subsequent years. It proved a perfect occasion for the Princess to inaugurate, not just the lights, but her career as a public figure in her own right.

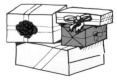

Princess Alice – a Christmas birthday

HRH Princess, Alice, Duchess of Gloucester, was born on Christmas Day 1901. Her father was the 7th Duke of Buccleuch. In November 1935 she married George V's third son Henry (HRH the Duke of Gloucester), at a private ceremony in the Chapel of Buckingham Palace. The Duke of Gloucester was a professional soldier and expected to make that his career. However he and his brothers were profoundly affected by the abdication of Edward VIII. The Duke of York became King George VI and the Duke of Gloucester gave up his army career to return to London and help his brother with his new duties.

Although she loves to spend time at her home, Barnwell Manor, near Peterborough, Princess Alice has always taken her full share of royal duties. During the war she was involved with the Red Cross, the St John Ambulance Brigade and what is now the WRVS. Since 1943 she has been head of the WRAF. From 1945-47, when the Duke was Governor General of Australia, the Princess was Commandant in Chief of the Australian Women's Land Army and of the three women's services.

Not surprisingly many of the organisations of which she is now Patron or President are connected with the armed forces. One of her main involvements is with BLESMA (The British Limbless Ex-Service Men's Association), of which she is Patron. This Association cares for service men and women permanently disabled as a result of service.

As part of BLESMA's 50th Jubilee celebrations a new rose, BLESMA Soul, was named in its honour. Because the Princess's birthday falls on Christmas Day it tends to go rather unnoticed, so on 6 January Lord Ancaster, the Society's late President, went to Kensington Palace to present the rose to her as a very special belated birthday gift. Despite the time of the year the Palace garden was bathed in sunshine and the Princess was clearly delighted to receive such beautiful roses in the middle of winter.

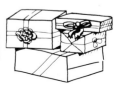

Children of courage

The Queen Mother was born with the new century and is now well into her ninth decade, yet she remains one of the busiest members of the Royal Family. Every year she fulfills a large number of engagements but one particular date in 1982 stood out among all the rest. On 15 December she attended a Christmas carol service in St Paul's Cathedral to honour fourteen very special children, the recipients of the 1982 Children of Courage Awards, sponsored by the magazine *Woman's Own*.

After the service the Queen Mother presented each child with a Scroll of Honour to commemorate the event. As she gave out the scrolls she was clearly deeply impressed by the individual stories and achievements which had earned the children their accolades. Some had overcome severe physical and mental handicaps, some had shown courage of a different kind by their fortitude during frightening accidents while others had saved the lives of family and friends. One had played amateur detective and brought about the arrest of five men after he had trailed a burglar for two

miles! Equally impressed were the many celebrities who had joined the children for the service, people like Lulu, Anthony Andrews, David Jacobs, Morecombe and Wise and Rod Hull and Emu.

The children had lunch at the House of Lords and in the afternoon they were given a guided tour of 10 Downing Street by Mrs Thatcher who gave each one a book and a box of chocolates. She paid them all a tribute saying 'We think you've done wonderful things and the future of our country is very safe as long as we have children like you.'

For all the adults involved it had been a moving and even a humbling experience. For the children it had been a day to remember all their lives and one made all the more special by the presence of the lady often known affectionately as 'the best loved granny in the world'.

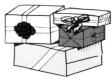

Not forgotten at Christmas

Because of the Duchess's Yorkshire background the Kents were married not at Westminster Abbey but at historic York Minster. The wedding was televised and millions of people were impressed by the Duke of Kent's beautiful blonde bride, in her flowing white dress. The Duchess's popularity has not wavered since her marriage. Perhaps one of the secrets of her success is that she has managed to retain an unaffected and unspoilt nature which comes across at every meeting and through every photograph.

The Duchess is Patron of The 'Not Forgotten' Association, which, as its title implies, was founded to make sure that disabled and wounded servicemen are not forgotten when they are no longer able to serve in the forces. Every year the Assocation holds Christmas parties throughout the country and the Duchess always tries to attend as many of these as possible. The most sought-after party is held at Buckingham Palace mews and it was this one which the Duchess visited just before Christmas 1984. She soon had the war veterans roaring with laughter as she tried on some of their party hats.

Apart from the 'Not Forgotten' Association the Duchess is also Patron of Age Concern, The Distressed Gentlefolks' Aid Association and the Spastics Society. In addition she is Chancellor of Leeds University in her native Yorkshire and this takes up a lot of her time. She relaxes by singing with the Bach Choir and despite her numerous commitments she tries to take part in as many of their concerts as possible. She is always particularly delighted when she is able to sing in their annual carol service at the Albert Hall.

Although it is her nature to become very involved with the organisation with which she is associated the Duchess's life revolves fundamentally around her home and family. She is deeply committed to the Christian ideal of family life, so that for her the Christmas season is probably more meaningful than to anyone else in the Royal Family.

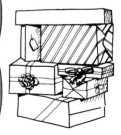

Princess Michael meets Santa

When Prince Michael married in 1978 his bride was very much an unknown quantity and their marriage presented several problems. Princess Michael is a Catholic, whose first marriage had been annulled. To marry her the Prince had to renounce his right of succession to the throne. Prince Michael wanted his children brought up as Anglicans so that their place in the line of succession would not be jeopardised. Because of this the Pope denied the couple the church wedding they wanted and it was several years before they received the church's seal of approval for their civil marriage.

After so many problems it would have been understandable if Princess Michael had tried to keep out of the public gaze. Instead she threw herself into the round of royal duties with an energy and zeal which surprised people. Prince Michael had always kept in the background but with his wife by his side he began to take on a far greater share of public duties, despite the fact that he gets no financial assistance from the civil list. The Princess has a friendly outgoing nature and always does everything she can to make any

public engagement a success. Among her many commitments she is a Trustee of the Victoria and Albert Museum, a reflection of her own interest in art and antiques. She runs her own interior design company, Szapar Designs Ltd, which specialises in the restoration of seventeenth and eighteenth century houses. It is not surprising therefore that the Prince and Princess chose to buy Nether Lypiatt Manor, a seventeenth century listed manor house in Gloucestershire. The Princess appears at many local functions and brings to these small affairs the same dash and verve that make her so sought after for major functions. It is fortunate that her personality is so vivacious as she could easily have found herself upstaged in the presence of both Father Christmas *and* Snoopy when she attended this Christmas fundraising fair in the small local town of Stroud.

Royal taste for pantomime

The Christmas pantomime is a perfect entertainment for members of the Royal Family, who all adore amateur theatricals. As well as the time-honoured tradition of after-dinner charades, at which Princess Margaret is probably one of the most competitive players, in recent years both Prince Charles and Prince Edward have become deeply involved with their college dramatic societies while at Cambridge. From the pictures of their productions it is clear that it is the comedy romp rather than deep tragedy which appeals to them most!

From 1941-44, while Princess Elizabeth and Princess Margaret were evacuated to the comparative safety of Windsor, an amateur pantomime was organised at the Castle each Christmas, in which the young Princesses took part with local children. The first of these pantomimes was Cinderella, with Princess Margaret in the title role and Princess Elizabeth as Principal Boy. The script was written by Mr Hubert Tanner the local schoolmaster, and seats were seven-and-six or five shillings, with proceeds to the Queen's Wool Fund.

Performances took place in the Waterloo Chamber where a stage had already been built for artistes invited down from London for Royal Command Performances. In 1943 the production was Aladdin, with Princess Elizabeth as Aladdin, Princess Margaret as Princess Roxana and a young lad from the Castle's Supply Department as Widow Twankey. Much of the laughter in this production revolved around references to the inordinate amount of laundry being sent down from the Castle together with the frequent, unexpected appearances of Aladdin himself from inside the laundry basket. The last of the Windsor pantomimes was put on for the Christmas season 1944/45. As usual it was scripted by the main participants and this time they invented a theme of their own, 'Old Mother Red Riding Boots' — an amalgam of traditional pantomime stories and nursery rhymes. This evocative production photograph shows 'The Hon. Lucy Fairfax' (Princess Margaret) and 'Lady Christina Sherwood' (Princess Elizabeth) mid performance, singing and tap dancing the number 'Swinging on a Star'.

Pantomime – a British tradition

Pantomime, like the Christmas card, is a British invention, but unlike the Christmas card it has not spread further afield. The pantomime developed from the Italian Harlequinade but by the mid-nineteenth century it had combined with the Music Hall to produce very much the format with which we are familiar today. Contemporary songs have always been a part of the pantomime which is very flexible within certain conventions. The stories all have a similar fairy-tale formula, an evil demon king (who appears from stage left), a good fairy (who appears from stage right), a beautiful Princess, her bumbling impecunious father, a lovable idiot, a handsome hero who is really a girl dressed up as a boy (who marries the girl who really is a girl) and a pantomime Dame who is of course a man dressed up as a woman (who would like to marry the man who is really a man who is the father of the girl who is really a girl). No wonder it confuses outsiders!

Queen Victoria loved the theatre and encouraged her family to mount amateur productions. At Christmas she and Prince Albert often took their children to seasonal shows, usually extremely elaborate productions with wild animals, casts of hundreds and complex mechanical sets which would be far too expensive to produce today.

When Victoria's children were young it was still customary to combine pantomime with the circus. There were several large circuses which toured the country, the greatest being 'Lord' George Sanger's circus. In London one particular theatre, Astley's, near Westminster Bridge, was really a circus which specialised in highly trained horses. At Christmas time pantomimes were staged there which combined the two traditions. These productions rejoiced in wonderful names like 'Harlequin Yankee Doodle Came to Town upon his Little Pony' (1849) and 'Paul Pry on Horseback' (1853). The Royal Family saw at least one of these spectacular productions. Quite often Victoria arranged for a performance to be given for her at Windsor. This picture shows Hengler's circus appearing before the Royal Family shortly after Christmas 1885.

Prince Philip – a pantomime president

Prince Philip is asked to be President or Patron of innumerable organisations. Since he likes to be actively involved with any organisation with which he is associated he tries to take on responsibilities which reflect his own interests and enthusiams. As a former officer in the Royal Navy he has many important Service appointments, including Admiral of the Fleet, Field Marshal and Marshal of the Royal Air Force. He is also Master of the Corporation of Trinity House, the general lighthouse authority for England and Wales.

The Prince's other appointments also underline his major interests. He believes in the importance of challenge and self-reliance for young people and for more than 25 years has been closely involved in the development and growth of the Duke of Edinburgh's Award Scheme. Since 1956 over two million young people have taken part in its challenging programme of community service, adventure and personal achievement.

The Prince is also concerned about the ecological problems facing the world with the advance of modern technology and has published several books on the subject. Since 1961 he has been associated with the World Wildlife Fund, first as UK President and now as International President. In 1970 he co-wrote 'Wildlife Crisis' with James Fisher and many of his speeches on the problems of protecting wildlife and preserving the ecological balance have also been published.

One of the ways in which he and other members of the Royal Family are able to help and support their favourite causes is by being present at fundraising events. Countless millions of pounds have been raised in this way. On 22 December 1983 Prince Philip was present at a Gala Performance of Aladdin at the Shaftesbury Theatre in London in aid of the National Playing Fields Association, of which he is President. The Prince enjoyed himself tremendously and entered totally into the pantomime spirit by joining in all the songs. The photograph shows him backstage after the performance, reliving some of the best moments with members of the cast, including Jill Gascoigne, Tommy Trinder, Lynsey de Paul, Derek Griffiths and Roy Kinnear.

Windsor wonderland

This beautiful and evocative picture of Windsor in the falling snow has a curiously timeless quality, although it was taken only a few years ago. Silhouetted in the foreground is Prince Philip driving a carriage and four.

Windsor Castle was initially built by William the Conqueror shortly after his memorable victory in 1066. Although built for strategic reasons it became a favoured royal residence in the middle ages because of the excellent sport offered by the surrounding deer forests. In the fourteenth century Edward III improved and embellished it and made it the headquarters of his chivalric order, The Order of the Garter. St George's Chapel, in the precincts of the Castle, is still the chapel of the Order, and the Garter Service is held there every year, usually on the Monday before the Royal Ascot race meeting.

Nearly every monarch who has lived at Windsor has made additions and improvements. The fairytale medieval atmosphere captured in this photograph is really a fantasy. Although the original structure dates back nearly a thousand years the picturesque battlements and crenelations were grafted onto the original by the architect Jeffry Wyatville in the early nineteenth century. Wyatville worked for George IV who, as Prince Regent, had spent a fortune on his Chinese-style palace at Brighton. The King spent even more money turning his real castle into a building which looked like his idea of a castle. The two men are responsible for the unified, gothic appearance of the building today.

Smith's Lawn, Windsor is the ideal location for Prince Philip's favourite sport, Competition Carriage Driving. He first became seriously involved in 1971, when arthritis in his right wrist forced him to give up polo. Since then he has become one of the best competitors in the world, taking part in two World Championships and helping Britain to win the gold medal in 1980. Success requires dedication and at Sandringham and Windsor the Prince takes every opportunity to practise, whatever the state of the weather!

Princess Alexandra's Christmas birthday

Like Princess Alice, Duchess of Gloucester, Princess Alexandra was born on Christmas Day. Princess Alexandra is the daughter of George V's fourth son, the Duke of Kent and his wife, Princess Marina of Greece. She was christened Alexandra after her great-grandmother Queen Alexandra but her last name, Christabel, is not a standard name in the Royal Family. It commemorates the day the Princess was born.

The Princess is renowned for her good humour and common sense. Unlike her cousins Elizabeth and Margaret, who were educated privately at home, Princess Alexandra went to school, the first royal Princess to do so. She and her brothers mixed freely with schoolfriends. This was very much the wish of Princess Marina who believed in a no-nonsense approach to child-rearing. Princess Alexandra has continued this attitude in her own life. She and her husband, Angus Ogilvy, have brought their children up with as little publicity as possible, and of course they have not inherited any titles.

The Princess's public engagements are always very relaxed, and she makes a point of speaking to as many people as possible. In 1984 she attended the National Playing Fields Association pantomime, as guest of honour, and seemed to enjoy it just as much as Prince Philip had done the year before. The pantomime, Jack and the Beanstalk, was at the Princess's local theatre on Richmond Green. The Princess and her husband are keen theatregoers and often go to the Richmond theatre privately, slipping in without any fuss. When her children were younger they were usually brought by their parents to see the pantomime, which has a reputation as one of the best traditional pantomimes in the country. Interestingly the Princess probably has a better view of the show when she attends privately than when she comes in her official capacity and sits in the royal box. Afterwards the Princess chatted for some time with the Dame, Kenneth Connor, and other members of the cast. Princess Alexandra's support helped the charity raise over £10,000 in one night.

A Christmas christening

In recent years most royal babies have been christened at Buckingham Palace. So the decision of the Prince and Princess of Wales to have Prince Harry christened at Windsor, four days before Christmas, came as something of a surprise. In the event combining the annual Christmas gathering of the entire Royal Family at Windsor Castle with a christening — surely the most appropriate family occasion to celebrate at Christmas — proved an inspired idea.

Prince Harry was christened Henry Charles Albert David in St George's Chapel on the Friday before Christmas, in front of a sizeable congregation from both sides of his family. He wore the traditional christening gown of fine Honiton lace made for Queen Victoria's first child, the Princess Royal. The silver gilt font decorated with lilies was the one designed by Prince Albert in 1841.

After the service Lord Snowdon took the official photographs. The relaxed and light-hearted pictures which resulted were due in no small part to the hilarious antics of two-and-a-half-year-old Prince William.

Described by his father as a 'spindly creature with a good sense of humour' he managed to keep everyone laughing. Millions of people were given a fascinating glimpse into life behind the scenes at a royal gathering when film of the christening party was shown as part of the Queen's Christmas Day broadcast. Prince William, playing hide-and-seek with his cousins Peter and Zara Phillips, seemed to be playing much the same role of court jester that he had done at the photo session.

The Queen's Christmas message has become an essential part of the Christmas festivities for millions, and it was an added bonus in 1984 to be allowed to join the Royal Family at one of their most private moments, at a time of the year which epitomises everything we most value in family life.

Brighton sleigh-bells

The Royal Pavilion at Brighton was built for the Prince Regent between 1815 and 1822 by the celebrated architect John Nash. Nash was responsible for the elegant classical style buildings which surround Regent's Park in London and the Royal Pavilion could hardly form a greater contrast. It is an extravagant mixture of Indian, Moorish and above all Chinese themes; a masterpiece which narrowly avoids being in appalling taste, and which was described by a contemporary as 'a little Kremlin'.

The Prince Regent (later George IV) adored Brighton and his increasingly elaborate, luxurious palace. It was the place to which he could escape from the cares and criticism of London.

George IV's niece, Queen Victoria, had very different opinions about the Royal Pavilion as a place of retreat. On her first visit, before her coronation, she wrote 'The pavilion is a strange, odd Chinese looking thing, both inside and outside'. Nevertheless the proximity of the sea did attract her. Unfortunately during later visits with her husband, Prince Albert, she was unable to enjoy the bracing sea air they both loved because of the unwelcome attentions of the crowd. 'We were mobbed by all the shopboys in the town, who ran and looked under my bonnet, treating us just as they do the Band, when it goes on parade'. This experience prompted Victoria and Albert to abandon Brighton and buy a country retreat of their own, Osborne, on the Isle of Wight.

This is a contemporary drawing of the Royal Family driving in their sleigh during their last visit to Brighton in 1845, when the town was covered by a thick fall of snow. The sleigh was pulled by two grey horses decorated with waving plumes and 'jingle bells'. The Queen and children sat in front wrapped up snugly in a fur rug while the Prince, an expert sleigh driver, stood at the back and a scarlet-clad escort rode alongside. The whole equipage provided an idyllic Christmas scene and it is hardly surprising that it attracted the crowds.

Family rooms at Windsor

Windsor Castle, where the Royal Family spends Christmas, is the country retreat of the Queen and her family. It is conveniently near London which makes it more suitable for weekends than Sandringham, it is large enough to accommodate an almost infinite number of guests, which makes it equally convenient for family Christmases and entertaining visiting Heads of State and there is still plenty of opportunity for riding and shooting despite the fact that it is a stone's throw from the M4 motorway and Heathrow airport.

Because of its history and royal associations the castle is a major tourist attraction. The State Apartments are open to the public. These apartments are magnificently decorated and hung with paintings by many of the Old Masters. Despite their names, 'The King's Drawing Room', 'The Grand Reception Room', 'The Queen's Audience Chamber' and so on, they are rarely used by the Queen. The last time the State Bedroom was used was in 1909! However the vast Waterloo Chamber which commemorates Wellington's victory, is the scene of many important State Banquets, and for Christmas lunch the State Dining Room is opened up in order to seat the entire family.

With so many sightseers the Queen has to guard her privacy. The Royal Apartments used by the Queen and her family are kept totally separate. They overlook the East Terrace, the sunken gardens, and the golf course built for Edward VII which Prince Philip uses as a helicopter pad.

To ensure their privacy the private apartments are never open to visitors and photographs of them are rare. This is the White Drawing Room, one of the Queen's private rooms, which she uses at weekends and at Christmas. It is quite homely in comparison with the grandeur of the State Apartments, the furniture is comfortable and there is a restful view of the countryside, making it an ideal place for the family to relax.

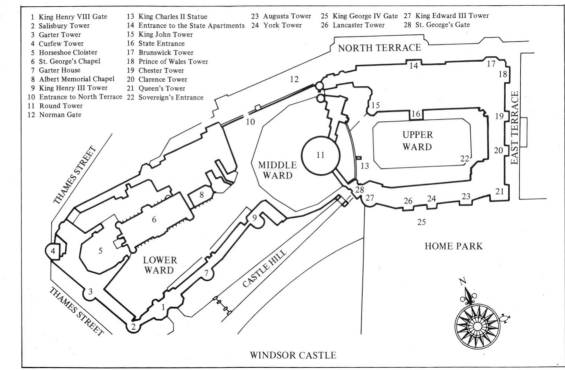

1 King Henry VIII Gate
2 Salisbury Tower
3 Garter Tower
4 Curfew Tower
5 Horseshoe Cloister
6 St. George's Chapel
7 Garter House
8 Albert Memorial Chapel
9 King Henry III Tower
10 Entrance to North Terrace
11 Round Tower
12 Norman Gate

13 King Charles II Statue
14 Entrance to the State Apartments
15 King John Tower
16 State Entrance
17 Brunswick Tower
18 Prince of Wales Tower
19 Chester Tower
20 Clarence Tower
21 Queen's Tower
22 Sovereign's Entrance

23 Augusta Tower
24 York Tower

25 King George IV Gate
26 Lancaster Tower

27 King Edward III Tower
28 St. George's Gate

NORTH TERRACE

EAST TERRACE

UPPER WARD

MIDDLE WARD

LOWER WARD

THAMES STREET

THAMES STREET

CASTLE HILL

HOME PARK

N

WINDSOR CASTLE

Christmas Eve at the castle

It is only since the war that Windsor has become the customary setting for Royal Christmases. Earlier in the century the usual Christmas residence was Sandringham. However, as a girl during the war the Queen grew to love Windsor and has happy memories of the Christmases she spent there. Also as the Royal Family has grown with the addition of new cousins and new generations Sandringham is no longer large enough to cope with the full complement, as the *entire* family likes to be together over the Christmas period.

The party begins to assemble a day or so before Christmas with the final guests arriving for lunchtime on Christmas Eve. Family presents are taken to the Red Drawing Room in the Brunswick Tower and set out on long tables, Victorian fashion, with children's presents grouped round a large tree at one end. There is another tree in the nursery quarters in the Queen's Tower. Not many years ago it would have been customary for all the children to stay there in the charge of their various nannies but times have changed. The children now stay in the same apartments as their parents and go over to the Queen's Tower for their meals and to play together. The younger children eat their Christmas lunch in the nursery as well.

The Queen herself decides where everyone is to stay, although there is now a fairly well-established order. For example, the Prince and Princess of Wales, with Prince William and Prince Harry, Prince Andrew and Prince Edward all stay in the Queen's apartments overlooking the East Terrace. Princess Anne and Captain Mark Phillips usually have the Augusta Tower nearby while the Gloucesters stay in the York Tower. Staff, too, has to be distributed rather inconveniently among the various towers; kitchen staff in the Brunswick Tower, footmen in King John's Tower, housemaids in Clarence Tower. Christmas at Windsor is indeed everyone's family Christmas writ very large indeed, and a triumph of organisation by the staff involved.

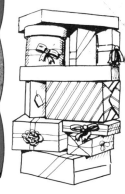

Church on Christmas morning

Nowadays Christmas often seems more like just another holiday for many people rather than a day with any religious significance. Despite the fact that the Royal Family also loves the chance to be together and enjoy all the entertainment the season has to offer it can never be without religious meaning for them, for the Queen is not just Head of State but also Head of the Church of England. Although this is a title which has been inherited by all English monarchs since the time of Henry VIII there is no doubt that the Queen takes the title very seriously indeed and is a deeply committed Christian.

There are several opportunities for church-going during Christmas at Windsor. There is a Midnight Mass in the main church in the precincts, St George's Chapel. The Queen does not usually attend this but the Duchess of Kent, a very active and involved member of the Anglican Church, may well attend. The general public is not admitted to this service which is only open to those who live in the Castle or Home Park, to people who work in the Castle or Chapel and to regular worshippers who are known to the Dean and Chapter. However the public are admitted to the Matins Service on Christmas morning. This is held at 10.45 and the Castle precincts and Chapel are open from 10 o'clock. There is room for about one thousand people so those that arrive in good time can be fairly sure of getting a seat. The entire Royal Family attends the Matins Service, except the very young children.

After the service the Queen lingers on the steps of the Chapel for a few minutes to chat with the Dean of Windsor. She and Prince Philip then return to the Queen's Tower by car, while some of the younger members of the party prefer a leisurely stroll back to work up an appetite for the traditional lunch which will be served at 1.15pm.

51

The Queen's private chapel

St George's Chapel at Windsor is an architectural gem which is famous all over the world. Less well known is the fact that the Queen also has a small private chapel in the Brunswick Tower, between the State Apartments and St George's Hall. It was built for Queen Victoria and is in the gothic style. The room itself is an unusual octagonal shape with an altar which stands in the window alcove and which can be curtained off. The chapel is completely lined with carved oak panelling decorated with medieval arches. From the high, elaborately decorated ceiling hangs an enormous gilt chandelier which is also gothic in style. In Queen Victoria's time the panelling was dark which, combined with the restricted light from the stained glass window, gave the chapel a somewhat gloomy air. In 1976 it was redecorated under the direction of the former President of the Royal Academy, the painter Sir Hugh Casson. Sir Hugh had overseen the interior design of the Royal Yacht Britannia and some of the private apartments at Windsor, which were long overdue for smartening up. Among the rooms he decorated was the visitor's suite in the Edward III Tower. His whole approach was to freshen and lighten the rather sombre interiors. In the chapel he succeeded by having all the woodwork painted a creamy white, and picking out the decorative detail in gold. The carpet was replaced with a very plain oatmeal colour and the wooden chairs, which are themselves decorated with gothic arches, were reupholstered in a gentle shade of pink. The effect is now very soft and restful.

Despite all the improvements the private chapel is not open to the public, but is occasionally used by the Queen and other members of the Royal Family. Early on Christmas morning a Communion Service is held there for anyone who cares to rise early. This service is open to any member of the staff who wishes to join in and quite a few of them like to attend before they begin their busy day.

The royal collection of paintings

This beautiful painting, *The Adoration of the Shepherds* by Jacopo Bassano is in the Royal Collection. It illustrates one of the incidents from the nativity described in the second chapter of St Luke's Gospel.

And it came to pass, as the angels were gone away from them into heaven, the shepherds said one to another, Let us now go even unto Bethlehem, and see this thing which is come to pass, which the Lord hath made known to us. And they came with haste and found Mary and Joseph, and the babe lying in a manger. And when they had seen it they made known abroad the saying which was told them concerning this child. And all they that heard it wondered at those things which were told them by the shepherds. But Mary kept all these things and pondered them in her heart.

This is just one of the many exquisite and priceless paintings in the Royal Collection. The collection has been built up over centuries by a succession of monarchs who were passionately interested in painting and works of art. Among the most assiduous and well-informed royal collectors were Charles I, who bought paintings by Rubens and van Dyck, Charles II who added the Leonardo da Vinci drawings, George III who bought many Canalettos to decorate Buckingham Palace and George IV, who added many Dutch Old Masters to the collection and patronised contemporaries such as Stubbs and Lawrence. Victoria and Albert both loved paintings and made presents of them to each other at birthdays and Christmas.

The Royal Collection is theoretically the Queen's collection, but is held by her in trust for succeeding generations. She and the Duke of Edinburgh have collected many modern paintings, including those of the Australian painter Sidney Nolan. However their greatest contribution has been undertaking the daunting programme of restoration and cataloguing which had become necessary after many years of neglect. Since 1962 the Queen has made the works of the Royal Collection available to the public in a constantly changing exhibition in the Queen's Gallery at Buckingham Palace.

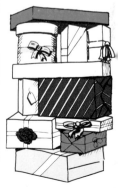

Christmas far from home

The Queen usually has the pleasure of celebrating Christmas surrounded by all her family at Windsor, and relishes the prospect just as much as Queen Victoria did. Very occasionally her schedule means that she finds herself far from home when Christmas comes around. This happened during Christmas 1953. After her coronation the Queen and the Duke of Edinburgh set out on a lengthy tour of the Commonwealth, to emphasise her commitment to the Commonwealth. On 20 December the royal couple were in Tonga enjoying a typical feast of coconut milk, suckling pig, yams and lobster in Queen Salote's feast house.

By Christmas Day itself they had moved on to New Zealand. New Zealand is still remarkably like Britain, for the majority of its three million people are descended from British immigrants. What is more, one of New Zealand's most famous personalities, Sir Edmund Hillary, had given an added zest to Coronation Day by becoming the first man to conquer Everest. Whereas in exotic Tonga is was easy to forget the time of year, in the homely atmosphere of New Zealand the royal couple must have been painfully aware that five-year-old Prince Charles and three-year-old Princess Anne would be missing them very much during their first Christmas apart.

Christmas Day was spent in Auckland, the New Zealand capital. The Queen attended a garden party at Government House and during the proceedings Father Christmas paid a call. Among the gifts he brought were a pram for Princess Anne and several other large, tempting packages for the royal children. Despite the jollity of the occasion, in this photograph the Queen seems just a little wistful and is clearly missing her own children as she watches Santa giving presents to the Governor General's two daughters. Four months later, at the end of the tour, Prince Charles and Princess Anne sailed on the maiden voyage of the Royal Yacht Britannia for a happy reunion with their parents at Tobruk, in North Africa, followed by a well-deserved holiday in Gibraltar and Malta.

Just an inexpensive trinket

The tiny mechanical elephant shown here was a Christmas present to George V from his family in 1929. It is made of gun metal with rubies for eyes and tusks made of ivory. On the underside is a small lever which starts it walking, nodding its head and swinging it tail from side to side.

The elephant was made by the renowned Russian jeweller Carl Fabergé (1846-1920). He lived at what was then called St Petersburg (now Leningrad) where his shop is still preserved. Although he worked in the most expensive materials it was not their value which chiefly interested him but the ingenuity and craftsmanship which he brought to his work. Many of his most famous pieces are executed in relatively inexpensive semi-precious stones. It is his exquisite workmanship which gives them their value.

Fabergé's pieces have been collected by the British Royal Family since the latter half of the nineteenth century, when Queen Alexandra, then the Princess of Wales, was introduced to his work by her sister, Princess Dagmar of Denmark, who had married the Tsar Alexander III of Russia. Enchanted by his designs Edward and Alexandra bought many pieces to give each other as presents. For Christmas 1907 the King arranged a special surprise for his wife, a complete set of all the animals to be found at their beloved Sandringham, including the Queen's favourite Pekinese dog, carved in the most lifelike manner out of semi-precious stones like jade, jasper and rose quartz.

Apart from his animal carvings Fabergé also specialised in miniature vases made from rock crystal apparently filled with water which contained stems of perfect flowers or fruit made from appropriately coloured metal or stones — purpurine for rowan berries or cherries, white quartzite for mock orange blossom, spun green gold for catkins. Because their love of Fabergé's work was well known items from his workshop were often given to Alexandra and Edward by their many wealthy friends. Alexandra always insisted that no present cost more than £50, but today the value of the collection is reckoned to be about five million pounds.

It's the thought that counts

Giving Christmas presents to the Royal Family genuinely poses the problem 'What do you give someone who has everything?' For George VI's family the question was to a large extent answered by the fact that the King had many interests and hobbies and was always glad to receive anything connected with them.

Like his parents and grandparents George VI collected Fabergé objects, especially cigarette cases for he was a heavy smoker. He was also a keen and well-informed stamp collector. The royal stamp collection is now probably the finest in the world. It was started early on in the history of postage stamps, 1856, when two of Queen Victoria's children, the Prince of Wales and Alfred, Duke of Edinburgh, visited a factory where the stamps were printed. The block of 6d. stamps presented to them became the basis of a new interest and the royal stamp collection had begun. George V was an even greater enthusiast than his father and his enthusiasm was passed on to his own son.

In 1949 George VI's wife, Queen Elizabeth, gave him a striking and unusual Christmas present which revealed many of the King's favourite pursuits. It was a glass casket, designed and engraved by Laurence Whistler, one of the foremost artists on glass of the twentieth century. The engravings around the sides represented some of the King's many interests. Several, such as music and painting, had to be abandoned for lack of room, but on the main panels of the final version Whistler has engraved designs to represent gardening, designing, shooting and reading. The right end panel represents the King's love of Scotland and the left end panel is a royal trophy. In the centre of the back panel the altar of love is represented. The initials E and G are entwined on it and watching over it is the God of Love. In the lid is engraved 'From the Queen to the King' and a poem by Whistler which concludes

> So may this page presume,
> though brief and small,
> To say what Love would say,
> and say it all.

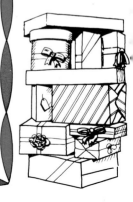

Albert had designs on Victoria

Prince Albert gave this set of jewellery to Queen Victoria for Christmas 1845 and for her birthday six weeks later. The Prince himself designed the enamelled gold and porcelain circlet, earrings and brooches. The five oranges hidden among the blossom represent their five children.

Prince Albert was an extremely gifted man with abilities in a wide range of spheres. Because the British government was suspicious of his influence and anxious not to let him become involved in policy matters he tended to channel his energies into the artistic, creative side of his nature. He and Victoria felt birthdays and Christmas were important opportunities to express their affection for one another and always took a great deal of trouble in choosing appropriate presents. Prince Albert often used the occasion to design the gifts himself and give British craftsmen the chance to demonstrate the extent of their skills. One particularly successful creation was a magnificent silver and gilt cake stand incorporating likenesses of all the Queen's dogs.

The Prince had a vision of combining art with all the advantages which the rapidly advancing technology of the Victorian age could offer. He was able to put his theories into practice in the two houses which he helped to design down to the smallest detail, Osborne on the Isle of Wight and Balmoral in the Scottish Highlands, where he oversaw the entire construction including the installation of bathrooms. At Balmoral the exterior sculpture, the furniture, the candelabra, supported by sculptures of highlanders in traditional kilts and bonnets, the carpets of Balmoral tartan which were used throughout the Castle, were all made to his design.

The culmination of Prince Albert's passion for combining design and science was the Great Exhibition of 1851, and the building which housed it, the Crystal Palace, was a perfect amalgam of art and engineering. The Great Exhibition greatly enhanced the prestige of Britain and of the Prince. Queen Victoria was quite accurate when she wrote in her diary the day it opened 'Albert's dearest name is immortalised by this *great* conception, *his* own.'

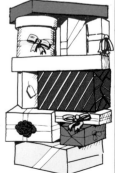

Enjoying the presents

After breakfast and before going to church members of the family have a chance to try out some of their presents. Prince Charles is seen here helping his younger brother, Prince Edward, to master the finer points of go-karting on the paths outside Windsor.

As can be seen from this picture, Prince Charles was very much a helpful older brother. The Queen has often referred to her younger children as 'my second family' for there is quite an age gap between Prince Charles and Princess Anne, both born soon after the Queen's marriage, and Prince Andrew and Prince Edward who were both born in the 1960s. Now the gap seems less obvious but fifteen years ago having much younger brothers must have been both a problem and a lot of fun for Prince Charles, who had got used to being the only son in the family. This photograph is unusual, for the Queen was very concerned to preserve the privacy of her second family, perhaps because she knew that their lives would be very different from that of Charles who will one day inherit the throne.

Of course go-karting was bound to appeal to Prince Charles who adores a challenge of any kind. Hardly a month goes by when he is not photographed trying out something different, ranging from parachute jumping and diving under the ice cap to disco-dancing and skate-boarding. Prince Edward too has gone out of his way to find excitement. He expects to join the Marines when he leaves Cambridge and during the holidays takes part in their gruelling training programme. Prince Andrew went straight into the navy on leaving school and quickly found more than his share of adventure on active service during the Falklands campaign.

It remains to be seen whether or not the new generation of Royal Princes will show the same spirit of adventure. However, Prince William, like Prince Charles as a child, has already been given a miniature working motor car, which will no doubt encourage him to take after his father.

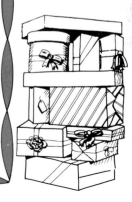

Easter eggs at Christmas

Queen Mary was a knowledgeable and avid collector of antiques. Like her mother-in-law, Queen Alexandra, she was not particularly interested in paintings but preferred curios and objets d'art, especially if they had some personal significance. She shared Queen Alexandra's passion for the work of Fabergé and added considerably to the collection kept in the main drawing room at Sandringham.

Fabergé had been forced to escape from Russia after the 1917 revolution, along with many of his wealthy clients. He settled in Paris but died shortly afterwards. After his death his work became even more sought after. Most of the aristocratic families which had fled in 1918 had managed to bring their valuables with them and these were gradually sold off to maintain their income. Queen Mary bought many items at these sales and her family added to her collection at Christmas and birthdays. One piece which reached her by an unusual route was a royal blue cigarette case encircled by a snake set with rose diamonds. This had been given to Edward VII by his mistress Mrs Keppel and on his death Queen Alexandra had returned it to her as a keepsake. Mrs Keppel herself gave it to Queen Mary to be kept with the rest of the Royal Collection.

The Easter egg shown here was bought by George V as a Christmas present for Queen Mary in 1933. These jewelled Easter eggs were Fabergé's most famous creations. Tiny (this one is 8.9 cms high) and perfect in every detail they opened up to reveal equally exquisite 'surprise' gifts inside. The Imperial Royal Family were Fabergé's best customers and Queen Mary managed to acquire two of their Easter eggs, which were especially interesting to her because of the family connection. The last Tsar, Nicholas II, was Queen Alexandra's nephew and his wife was Queen Victoria's granddaughter. In 1934 George V and Queen Mary bought the best-known Easter egg of the Imperial Collection. Given to the Tsarina by Nicholas II in 1914, it contains a miniature screen painted in enamel with the profiles of their five children.

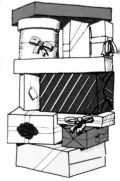

Christmas at Osborne

Because of Windsor's unhappy associations with the death of Prince Albert, Queen Victoria, in her old age, took to spending Christmas at Osborne. Christmas there followed all the traditions and customs which had evolved when her children were small, including the trees decorated with gingerbread men, and long tables covered with presents for every member of the family and the household. These tables were set out in the Durbar Room. The scene is described by Bernard Mallet, whose wife Marie was one of Queen Victoria's Maids of Honour and whose diaries were later published by their son. 'After tea was summoned with the household to the Durbar Room to see the Royal presents set out on long tables round the room. The Queen in her chair was wheeled round to see her presents and examine everything with the most evident and lively interest and pleasure — a pretty and touching sight.'

We are fortunate to have a contemporary photograph of the Durbar Room taken at Christmas 1986. Among the gifts are many paintings and photographs. Queen Victoria's reign virtually coincided with the invention of photography and photographs proved an invaluable addition to her own sketches and diaries to record the day to day detail of the Queen's family life. Even today the homes of members of the Royal Family tend to be crammed with family photographs.

The Durbar Room is a remarkable example of interior decoration. Added to Osborne in 1890, it expresses the Queen's own taste without the influence of Prince Albert. She never actually visited India, although she was proclaimed Empress of India, but she loved every aspect of its culture. She kept Indian servants at court and woe betide anyone who treated then with less than perfect courtesy. She learned to speak Hindustani and constantly urged her colonial representatives to work for greater understanding of the Indian culture. The Durbar Room was designed by Rudyard Kipling's father and an Indian, Bhai Ram Singh. The Queen used it for receptions and for displaying the presents and tributes sent to her from India.

"This perfect little paradise"

Prince Albert and Queen Victoria were looking for a country residence with real seclusion when they heard that Osborne House on the Isle of Wight was for sale. This watercolour of the original house was painted by C. R. Stanley in October 1844 when the Queen visited Osborne to see if it would suit her. Indeed the location did suit her very well. The house had wonderful views across the Solent, extensive grounds to ensure privacy and its own private beach. Queen Victoria wrote to her uncle, the King of the Belgians, 'You will, I am sure, be pleased to know that we have succeeded in purchasing Osborne, in the Isle of Wight . . . It sounds so nice to have a place of one's own, quiet and retired, and free from all Woods and Forests, and other charming Departments who really are the plague for one's life.'

Unfortunately the charming eighteenth-century house seen here proved too small for Victoria's growing family and the members of the household who had to accompany her, so plans were soon afoot to pull it down and rebuild. This was a project dear to the heart of the Prince

Consort who planned an Italian-style villa with two large towers. He became totally involved in all the detail of the building and furnishing of Osborne and he and his wife were delighted with it when they finally moved in in 1846. One of the features which pleased them most was the division of the building into separate blocks for the family and for the household. The gardens were landscaped in terraces going down to the sea and well planted with large trees to ensure the maximum privacy. Osborne proved ideal for the children, who spent their summer holidays there. It became part of the family's routine to visit Osborne after Christmas, just as the present Royal Family goes to Sandringham. It was in this 'perfect little paradise' that Queen Victoria made her celebrated remark 'We are not amused' to reprimand a dinner guest who had overstepped the mark.

Christmas fare

Nowadays we think of roast turkey, followed by Christmas pudding, as the traditional Christmas meal. However turkeys were not brought to England until the sixteenth century. In the early middle ages a royal Christmas feast would have been made up of the highly-spiced stews and 'messes' served at all great feasts. The centrepieces of the long tables were the 'subtleties' which were the culmination of the medieval pastry cook's art. Intended to be looked at rather than eaten, 'subtleties' were incredibly elaborate sculptures of castles, birds, or mythical beasts. Frequently they were gilded with real gold and decorated with costly jewels. The most prestigious main courses were a highly decorated boar's head or a peacock served in its own feathers. Even to this day boar's head is found as part of an elaborate buffet meal. However it lost some of its importance as part of the Christmas feast during the reign of James I (1603-1625) who loathed pork in any form.

Nowadays the Royal Family's Christmas lunch as Windsor is familiar turkey and pudding. However, until the second half of the twentieth century it was a far more elaborate affair. This can be seen even in the comparatively light meal described by Maria Mallet's husband during their Christmas at Osborne: 'Baron of beef, woodcock pie from the Lord Lieut. of Ireland, boar's head displayed on sideboard.'

In 1841-1842 the Chief Cook and Maitre d'Hotel to Queen Victoria was Charles Elmé Francatelli, who was of Italian origin, and had trained in France. When he left the Queen's service, he was able to capitalise on the reputation of his former job. He published several cookery books which became best sellers because of their royal connections. Foremost of these was 'The Modern Cook' published in 1846. The recipe for woodcock pie, eaten by the royal party at Osborne, is the one given by this royal chef.

Francatelli's 'Pie of Woodcocks à L'Irlandaise'

Pick the birds clean, cut off the legs and wings, singe them, and then cut each woodcock into halves: remove the gizzards, leaving the trail, and set them aside on a plate. Then, cover the sides and bottom of a white glazed earthen oval pan (used for preserving game) with very thin layers of fat bacon, place the woodcocks in the pan in close layers, each well-seasoned with ground black pepper and salt, and a small proportion of prepared aromatic spices. When this is done, fill up the pan with a sufficient quantity of clarified fresh butter to cover the birds, place some layers of fat bacon on the top, cover the pan hermetically with a firm flour-and-water paste: bake the pie in a moderately-heated oven for about two hours; when it has become cold, remove the crusts, wash the edges and sides of the pan, and run a little fresh clarified butter on the top; when cold, ornament with a neat border of pickled double parsley, set the pie on a folded napkin laid on its dish, and serve.

This is perhaps the best method of making pies of woodcocks or snipes, as from the simplicity of the ingredients used, the birds retain their flavour: an important consideration with amateurs of this kind of game.

Christmas cake

Public engagements can sometimes be rather a serious business but there are also plenty of light-hearted occasions like this. Here Prince Charles is about to sample a Christmas cake, one of many being prepared for the Christmas season, at a bakery he visited. Offered endless hospitality nearly every day the Royal Family have developed the ability to avoid the worst excesses without upsetting people's sensibilities. It is well known that they prefer plain, simple food and if this is not available one of the most reliable methods of cutting down on calories is to push their food round the plate rather than tucking in.

But Christmas at Windsor, as it is in less stately homes, is a day for forgetting rigid self discipline for a while. After a short afternoon walk in the grounds everyone returns for tea, which includes a vast Christmas cake made by the Queen's own pastry chef. The recipe for Christmas cake given here was written over one hundred years ago, a fact reflected in the price of the finished article!

CHRISTMAS CAKE

Ingredients. — 5 teacupfuls of flour, 1 teacupful of melted butter, 1 teacupful of cream, 1 teacupful of treacle, 1 teacupful of moist sugar, 2 eggs, ½oz. of powdered ginger, ½lb. of raisins, 1 teaspoonful of carbonate of soda, 1 tablespoonful of vinegar.

Mode. — Make the butter sufficiently warm to melt it, but do not allow it to oil; put the flour into a basin, add to it the sugar, ginger and raisins, which should be stoned and cut into small pieces. When these dry ingredients are thoroughly mixed, stir in the butter, cream, treacle, and well-whisked eggs, and beat the mixture for a few minutes. Mix the soda with the dry ingredients, being very careful to leave no lumps, and stir the vinegar into the dough. When it is wetted, put the cake into a buttered mould or tin, place it in a moderate oven immediately, and bake it from 1¾ to 2¼ hours.

Average Cost, 1s. 6d.

Origins of Christmas pudding

For the famous English Christmas pudding, we are largely indebted to an eighteenth century monarch, George I. He came over to Britain from Hanover and never lost his preference for everything German, especially German women and German food. The English had always shown a liking for suety food, particularly in the winter, and their love of sweet things was legendary. In the reign of Elizabeth I it was the English who bought up almost the entire production of dried fruit from Southern Europe. By the eighteenth century British chefs specialised in rich puddings with strange names, such as trifle, whim-wham and floating islands. George I's new subjects were therefore ready and willing to adopt the sweet, fruity German suet puddings, making them virtually their most famous national dish. A French visitor during George I's reign wrote, 'Ah, what an excellent thing is an English pudding! To come in Pudding Time, is as much as to say, to come in the most Lucky Moment in the World.'

At that time, right up to the early twentieth century, Christmas pudding was usually known as plum pudding, because it is rich in raisins, which were then called plums. Like Christmas fruit cake, plum pudding made a perfect nourishing mid-winter dish. It was also an opportunity to cheer everyone up by being lavish with some of the winter's store of dried and preserved provisions half-way through the bleak season, when the cook had a good idea of how well supplies were going to last.

Prince Albert, who so loved and fostered the Christmas traditions, also loved his native German cuisine. Chefs named many dishes in his honour, including a suet pudding. The rich pouring custard usually served with steam puddings came to be known as German custard sauce. Queen Victoria's chef, Francatelli, naturally included recipes for plum pudding and its accompanying sauce in his book, 'The Modern Cook'.

Francatelli's Plum Pudding

INGREDIENTS:– Three-quarters of a pound of raisins, three-quarters of a pound of currants, half a pound of candied orange, lemon, and citron, one pound and a quarter of chopped beef suet, one pound of flour, three-quarters of a pound of moist sugar, four eggs, about three gills of milk, the grated rind of two lemons, half an ounce of nutmeg, cinnamon, and cloves (in powder), a glass of brandy, and a very little salt.

Mix the above ingredients thoroughly together in a large basin several hours before the pudding is to be boiled; pour them into a mould spread with butter, which should be tied up in a cloth. The pudding must then be boiled for four hours and a half; when done, dish it up with a German custard-sauce spread over it.

German Custard Sauce

Put four yolks of eggs into a *bain-marie* or stewpan, together with two ounces of pounded sugar, a glass of sherry, some orange or lemon peel (rubbed on loaf sugar), and a very little salt. Whisk this sharply over a very slow fire, until it assumes the appearance of a light frothy custard.

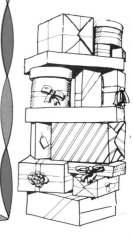

The Queen's speech

At 3 o'clock on Christmas Day the Royal Family, like every family in the land, switches on the television to watch the Queen's speech. When Elizabeth II came to the throne the Christmas radio broadcast, made live by the monarch after lunch on Christmas Day, was an integral feature of Christmas in the United Kingdom and the Commonwealth. This was emphasised by the Queen's first broadcast on Christmas Day 1952. 'Each Christmas, at this time, my beloved father broadcast a message to his people in all parts of the world. Today I am doing this to you, who are now my people. As he used to do I am speaking to you from my own home, where I am spending Christmas with my family: and let me say at once that I hope your children are enjoying themselves as much as mine are on a day which is especially the children's festival, kept in honour of the Child born at Bethlehem nearly two thousand years ago.'

The televising of the Coronation the following year sent sales of television sets rocketing and it was soon clear that television had ousted radio as a means of communication. So in 1957 the Queen made her first televised Christmas speech, which was broadcast live. Very understandably the prospect of making a live appearance rather dampened the relaxed atmosphere of family Christmas lunch and it came as a great relief when, in 1960, the Queen was able to pre-record her speech, as she has done ever since.

Although she is advised by experienced television technicians the nature of her broadcast is entirely the Queen's decision. She regards it as an invaluable opportunity to emphasise ideals, such as Commonwealth unity, which she sees as important, and which often seem to get pushed into the background. For the public the most welcome innovation she has made has been the gradual introduction of informal film of her family, making them seem much closer and more accessible.

The first Christmas broadcasts

The innovator of the Christmas broadcast was the Queen's grandfather, King George V. Public radio broadcasting had been set up by the BBC in 1922 and George V was quick to see the possibilities for communicating 'personally' with more of his people than had ever been dreamed of. He made his very first broadcast in 1924 when he opened Wembley stadium and in the following year broadcast from Wembley again when he opened the British Empire Exhibition. This speech was somewhat marred by the rattle of hailstones hitting the roofs of the stands! In 1932 he made his first Christmas Day broadcast, choosing 3 o'clock as the most suitable time, a time which has remained unchanged for over fifty years. In 1934 the Royal Family was at Sandringham for Christmas when the King made what many feel was his most effective broadcast, relishing the novelty of communicating with the whole world from a small corner of Norfolk.

As I sit in my own home I am thinking of the great multitudes who are listening to my voice, whether they be in British homes or in far off regions of the world. For you all, and especially for your children, I wish a happy Christmas.

By this time broadcasting had become an integral part of life for the Royal Family. The home-made Christmas card on the left shows how aware even the youngest were of the importance of communication. Set into the hand-decorated mount is a photograph of the Queen as a young girl making her first ever broadcast with Princess Margaret. It was sent to Queen Mary as a Christmas card in 1941.

The ability to adapt to change and use it to advantage, as George V did when he saw the benefits of using radio, is one of the great strengths of the Royal Family in the twentieth century. Since that first broadcast in 1932 the Christmas speech has become as much a part of our traditional Christmas as Christmas trees and Christmas pudding.

Evening parlour games

After supper on Christmas Day the Royal Family likes to stay up late and play Charades. The true Victorian game of Charades, so delightfully illustrated here by Queen Victoria, is really a short three-act play, with script and costumes, in which syllables are introduced to make up a final word or phrase which is given in its entirety in the last scene. This example from a nineteenth-century book of Parlour Games shows how the actors can surreptitiously introduce the first syllable of the phrase 'Go-Bang'.

The curtain drawn aside. Miss Jenkyns is seen reclining on her drawing-room couch, with a weary look on her face and a book in her hand.

Enter Footman
Footman (pulling his forelock). — 'Please ma'am, I'm come to say I wish to give you notice; I can't stop here no longer!'
Lady. — 'Why, James, how is this? What can have made you so unexpectedly come to this decision?'

James. — 'Well, ma'am, you see I want to live where there are more carriage visitors. I have nothing at all to say against you, ma'am, or the place; but I want to better myself by seeing a little of 'igh life.'
Lady. — 'Then if you have no other reason for wanting to *go*, James, I fear we shall have to part, as I certainly can't arrange to receive carriage visitors simply for your benefit.'
(Sinks languidly back on the couch and resumes her book. James retires.)
Lady (to herself). — 'How tiresome these servants are, to be sure, now I shall have the trouble of engaging a new footman. I really think no one with my delicate health had ever so much to do before.'
(Rises and retires.)'

P. 17. Oct. 30th 1832.

Rigsby?

Last scene of the charade at Chatsworth.

Kenilworth

The Boxing Day shoot

Unless Boxing Day falls on a Sunday, the men of the Royal Family spend the day shooting in the grounds of Windsor Castle. Hunting and shooting are royal pastimes which go back literally a thousand years to a time when the Kings had to hunt to eat. In the middle ages all the forests in the country, and the animals in them, belonged to the King. Windsor was famous for its deer forests and therefore a popular residence with all the medieval monarchs, while Richmond Park in London was once a royal hunting park. Although there is no longer any need to hunt in order to eat, shooting remains a popular royal sport, partly through tradition and partly because so many men in the Royal Family have been trained in the armed forces and welcome the chance to put their marksmanship to the test. Most of the women in the family are also competent shots. One of the reasons for the Boxing Day shoot is that it gives the opportunity for fresh air and exercise after the indulgences of the day before, even if the sport offered by the Windsor estate is no longer what it was. Lately the Royal Family has become aware that not

everyone in the country approves of shooting as a sport and Prince Charles has been markedly absent on recent occasions. This may be partly due to the influence of the Princess of Wales who does not enjoy shooting. On Boxing Day 1984 she and Prince Charles went for a brisk walk instead of joining the shoot.

However Prince Andrew, reminiscent in this photograph of Edward VII, in his tweed suit, preferred to go along with tradition. The relationship of man and dog is one of the most satisfying aspects of shooting. Labradors, like the one with Prince Andrew, are bred on the royal estate at Sandringham, and brought up to Windsor when required. One particularly successful working labrador was George VI's dog, Windsor Bob, which came first in the Kennel Club's retriever trials in 1948.

Boxing Day entertainment

While they are out shooting on Boxing Day the Queen's party is served with lunch at the Village Hall in Windsor Great Park. A typical shooting lunch is taken over in advance in polythene containers and set out formally like a very grand picnic. It consists of dishes such as glazed lamb cutlets, lobster salad and a variety of fresh salads, followed by cheese and coffee, with wine and spirits for those that want them. Having the family out of the way for the day gives the Windsor staff a chance to relax and get things straight after the demanding schedule of Christmas Day.

As the light starts to fade the shooting party returns to the Castle where tea is served. Everyone then disappears to rest, bathe and change before dinner which is served at 8.15pm. On Boxing Night the after-dinner entertainment is always a film, which is shown in the grandeur of the Garter Throne Room. This room, lined with portraits of sovereigns in their Garter robes, is in the oldest part of the Castle. Here the Knights of the Garter gather in June for the Queen to invest new Knights.

The Queen has a travelling cinema — projection equipment and full-size screen — which can be taken to any of her residences. The Garter Throne Room has been designed so that the canopy above the throne can be rapidly dismantled to reveal a projection room. The screen is set up at the opposite end of the long room, the chairs are re-arranged, and hey presto Windsor Castle has its own cinema.

Film companies supply the Queen with brand new pre-release films, so there is no chance of anyone being bored by a film they have already seen. The film is chosen carefully to be good family entertainment, in case any of the children get to stay up late and watch it. Past favourites include the James Bond movies and the Pink Panther films, starring a great royal favourite, Peter Sellers.

After the film Boxing Day is rounded off with drinks and sandwiches served in the Oak Drawing Room.

...and a Happy New Year

The illustration on the left is a miniature concertina calendar sent by Queen Victoria to Queen Mary for Christmas 1895 to help her plan the New Year.

For the present Royal Family New Year is the time to move from Windsor to Sandringham in Norfolk. The house party at Windsor usually stays on for another day's pheasant shooting after Boxing Day and then breaks up. The Queen, the Duke of Edinburgh and the Queen Mother invariably go to Sandringham but the remainder of the party varies from year to year. The Duke and Duchess of Kent usually go to their country house, Anmer Hall, which is a few miles down the road from Sandringham. Prince Edward and Prince Andrew will accompany their parents for part of the holiday but Prince Charles and Princess Anne may return to their own homes in Gloucestershire. Prince and Princess Michael of Kent also go back to Gloucestershire. The Princess has become a keen horsewoman in the last few years and likes to make the most of the hunting season with the local hunt, the Beaufort.

The Queen's father, grandfather and great-grandfather all celebrated Christmas at Sandringham. George V and George VI then stayed on to enjoy the shooting. George V in particular was almost obsessed by shooting and was a brilliant marksman. In later years he was always accompanied by his favourite black labrador, Sandringham Simon. Edward VII was also a fine shot and was responsible for making the shooting offered at Sandringham some of the finest in the country, but after Christmas he preferred to return to London and the glittering social round of parties and theatre which was such an important part of his life. When Elizabeth II came to the throne she took over her father's routine and was at Sandringham for her first televised Christmas broadcast. However she eventually developed her own way of doing things. The Queen is renowned for liking a set routine and now Christmas at Windsor and New Year at Sandringham together with summer at Balmoral, have become immovable feasts.

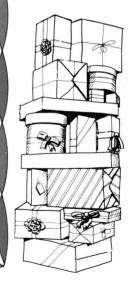

Sandringham at Christmastide

Sandringham, seen here covered in snow, was the scene of many of the Queen's early childhood Christmases. Her grandfather, George V, loved the house his father had built. While Edward VII was alive George V and Queen Mary, then Prince and Princess of Wales, lived at York Cottage, a short walk from the main house, They spent their honeymoon there, and although Queen Mary, who had the responsibility of keeping the household running smoothly, found it small and overcrowded, George V loved the simplicity of the life there and was happy to allow his mother to stay on at the main house after her husband's death. He and Queen Mary did not move in there until 1925.

As their grandchildren were born George V and Queen Mary were delighted to be able to welcome all their family for Christmas at Sandringham. (In 1935 the Princes caused quite a stir by arriving, together with their luggage and presents, in their own aeroplanes!) Princesses Elizabeth and Margaret were there for Christmas with their parents. Their cousins the sons of the Princess Royal, Countess of Harewood, came down to join them for the New Year. Queen Mary used to choose the finest fir tree she could find in the Sandringham plantation and set it up in the ballroom. She herself decorated the tree and the servants received their Christmas presents from it. The young Princesses were given theirs after breakfast on Christmas morning. Nowadays the ballroom is also the scene of the Sandringham staff's Christmas party and is used for the travelling cinema which is brought with the rest of the Queen's luggage from Windsor.

In the afternoon George V and Queen Mary entertained their grandchildren with old-fashioned games like blind man's buff and musical chairs. Both of them found it easier to be relaxed and informal with their grandchildren than with their own children.

It is now possible for the public to visit the scene of these past Christmas festivities as Sandringham is open to visitors for part of the year.

"Dear old Sandringham"

This photograph of Sandringham in the frost taken at New Year 1889 is a perfect complement to the modern snow-covered scene on the previous page. Sandringham was bought by Queen Victoria for her son, the future Edward VII, in 1862. The original house quickly proved too small after his marriage to Princess Alexandra of Denmark in 1863, and plans were made to extend it. Several lodges were built in the grounds to house staff and guests, including Bachelor's Cottage, which was renamed York Lodge when the Duke and Duchess of York (George V and Queen Mary) lived there. Eventually instead of adding piecemeal to the house it was decided to demolish it all, except for the conservatory, which became a billiard room, and rebuild. The new house was very different from the one Princess Alexandra was taken to in 1863 but shortly after this photograph was taken further changes had to be made. The Prince nearly always celebrated his birthday at Sandringham, and on 1 November 1891, a week before his guests arrived for the birthday celebrations, the house caught fire. It was probably the result of a defective chimney and was made more lethal by the layers of sawdust with which the bedroom walls were packed to reduce noise. Undeterred, Edward went ahead with his party under a temporary tarpaulin roof, but the house needed extensive repairs. While these were being done a new East Wing was added.

All the succeeding monarchs have loved Sandringham as much as Edward did and have made improvements. To George V it was 'Dear Old Sandringham, the place I love better than anywhere else in the world.'

He loved the informality, with Queen Mary presiding over the teapot while tea was served in the entrance hall. To increase its privacy he bought up several of the neighbouring estates as they became available. The Queen loves Sandringham as much as any of her predecessors, but for her the most enticing feature is that sections of the Queen's Thoroughbred Stud are kept there. During her reign Sandringham and its estate have become entirely self supporting.

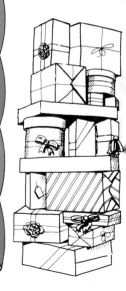

Queen Alexandra's Christmas

Queen Alexandra was always happiest at Sandringham. When Edward brought her to the house as a young bride of eighteen the flat, windswept countryside reminded her of her native Denmark and she chose to remain there as a widow from 1910 until her death in 1925. Edward loved the house for the shooting and because it allowed him to be a generous and expansive host. Alexandra loved it because it was the nearest she got to an ordinary home life with her husband and the five children she adored. Edward was a devoted and approachable father not remote as so many men at the time were to their children. The habit of spending Christmas at Sandringham and making it a cosy family time was especially important to Alexandra because as the years went by she and Edward spent less and less time together.

Known as 'Motherdear' Queen Alexandra was an intensely fond mother who remained close to her children even when they had grown up. George V was devoted to her. While he was away with the navy they corresponded frequently. At Christmas 1889 he was away at sea and Alexandra wrote to him.

how dreadfully I missed you for Xmas. There were all the tables excepting yrs. & there were all the cheery voices excepting the cheeriest of all & yr. bright little face with its turned up snout oh I did miss it & really shed a little secret tear for my Georgie dear.

The painting shown here hangs in the lobby at Sandringham and can be seen by visitors to the house. It is by an artist called Karl Bauerle and was painted in January 1871. It depicts Edward and Alexandra during their happiest period as a family, skating and sleighing with their children on the ice-covered lake at Sandringham during the Christmas holiday.

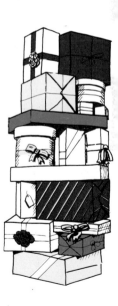

Country sports for New Year

This picture of Prince Charles out shooting pheasants in January 1985 gives an impression of the scale and bleakness of the countryside around Sandringham. It is possible to go out shooting for fourteen days in succession and not cover the same ground twice. Edward VII took positive steps to improve the shooting at Sandringham by careful stocking with pheasants and partridges and by introducing back into the wild birds which had been hand-reared. During his time the birds shot in a season were counted in tens of thousands. So keen was the King on the sport that clocks were actually kept half an hour faster than standard time to allow the maximum amount of shooting during the short winter days. This was known as Sandringham time and was not discontinued until his grandson, Edward VIII's brief reign in 1936. Since 1939 game birds have no longer been hand-reared at Sandringham. The continuing supply is dependent on the careful management of wild birds, giving them the optimum conditions for successful breeding and keeping down the animals which prey on

them. This is what Prince Charles meant in his apparently paradoxical statement 'Because you kill animals doesn't mean that you don't appreciate them fully or want to conserve them.'

However, shooting is not the only sport available at Sandringham. The Queen herself takes the opportunity to ride as much as possible and has even given the Princess of Wales some lessons. Prince Philip finds the terrain excellent for training his carriage-driving team, and it is rumoured that he will use Sandringham as a base to help other competitors when he eventually retires from competition. He may set up a school for teaching others interested in what he considers to be an unjustly neglected sport.

Those who are less committed or energetic can simply enjoy walking in the bracing fresh Norfolk air or a gentle stroll around the gardens, one of the pleasures of a royal Christmas which can be shared by any of the many visitors who now visit Sandringham each year.

A month in the country

The Sandringham estate has grown considerably since Sandringham Hall was purchased for Edward VII. Outlying estates were bought up as they became vacant, and land has been reclaimed from the Wash. The Queen owns the estate privately and takes a personal interest in each of the seven villages which now make it up. These villages include Dersingham from which Sandringham (Sant Dersingham) derives its name. While she is at Sandringham the Queen attends church every Sunday and goes to a different village in turn. St Peter's is the church on the original Sandringham estate and is often called Sandringham Church. The other churches she attends are at Wolferton and West Newton which are both a short drive away. Those who do not live in Norfolk are not really aware of how much the Queen is regarded as a much-loved local landowner. Because the Royal Family have been locals for so many years the people in the surrounding villages are intensely loyal and even a little proprietorial about the Queen and her family. Every Sunday morning there is always a good sized crowd outside the church where she

is due to worship, and she is often given bouquets and small bunches of flowers from the children. On one occasion the small boy proffering his flowers became rather clumsy in his excitement and managed to bump her on the nose with them. The Queen was not the least bit cross but she did look a little surprised.

In this photograph, taken on 3 February 1985, shortly before the end of their Christmas holiday, the Queen and Prince Philip are seen chatting with the Vicar as he escorts them through the churchyard at West Newton. Prince Philip is clearly highly amused by one of the Vicar's remarks. It is all rather reminiscent of the scene outside St George's Chapel, Windsor on Christmas morning, but much more informal. The informality and unvarying warmth of their reception are among the reasons the Royal Family find their visit to Sandringham such a truly relaxing way to finish off their Christmas holiday.

Rural pursuits

The six weeks at Sandringham is intended as a holiday break in the Queen's busy schedule and she unwinds during the time she spends there. However a glance at the local newspapers soon makes it clear that it is not a time when the Queen refuses all public engagements – far from it. The regard and affection which the local people have for her is reciprocated and the Queen takes advantage of her time at Sandringham to keep up her local connections and to carry out visits almost as a local personality rather than Queen.

It has always been customary for the royal ladies to show their support of rural life and organisations by being members of the local Sandringham WI. Queen Mary became Honorary President of the Norfolk Federation of Women's Institutes back in 1919. While at Sandringham the Queen always attends at least one meeting, as does the Queen Mother, the current Honorary President. If Princess Margaret joins the Sandringham house party before holidaying at her house on the Caribbean island of Mustique, she too joins her mother and sister. On 26 January 1977 all three were present at the meeting at West Newton Village Hall when this photograph was taken. They saw an exhibition of brass and copper, to which the Queen Mother had contributed a brass lion, and heard a talk on spooky tales and haunted houses. Occasionally the Queen herself gives a talk about her travels during the year; in 1983 she spoke about her visit to the Commonwealth Games. The highlight of the meeting is tea. This is served at tables for four and each of the royal party presides at a table. Each year different members get the chance to sit and have their tea poured for them by the Queen. This is done on a rota basis, based on alphabetical order of names. Everything is done to make the meeting just like any other and when the two hours is over the Queen slips quietly away without any fuss.

The frozen fens

For children a Christmas holiday is perfect if there is plenty of snow. This photograph was taken at Sandringham in January 1971, when Prince Edward was only six years old. It shows the Prince hiding from his brother Prince Andrew during a particularly boisterous game of snowballing. The heavy snow which fell in January 1985 gave Prince William, who was staying at Sandringham, the chance to build his first snowman, with a little help from his seven-year-old cousin Peter Phillips.

Sandringham is a good base for anyone who likes winter sports, for East Anglia bears the brunt of the cold weather coming across the continent from as far away as Siberia. The nearby fenland freezes over in really cold weather and makes a perfect natural skating rink. Many religious refugees from Holland settled in the fenland area in the sixteenth century because of its similarity with their own country and they taught the local people the sport they practised on their own fenlands. Like true Norfolk locals Edward VII and Alexandra loved to skate whenever the weather was right. They organised wonderful skating parties on the lakes at Sandringham with plenty of hot spiced wine to keep their guests warm and cheerful. Princess Alexandra was considered a particularly expert skater and always cut a fine figure on the ice, her tall graceful figure well wrapped up in furs. Guests who could not skate were not left out of the fun but were pushed around the ice in special chairs. Edward himself, although he lacked his wife's grace, was an expert skater, having been taught by his father Prince Albert, who also taught him and his brothers and sisters how to play ice hockey. The ice hockey tradition was continued by George VI who organised a Sandringham team to play against a team from the American air base during the Second World War. The Queen's children have all learned to skate and Prince Andrew played ice hockey during his stay at Lakefield College, Ontario.

Dressing up warmly

In theory the Royal Family takes six weeks complete holiday in the New Year but in practice the round of public engagements begins to gather pace early in the New Year. Princess Alexandra, refreshed by her combined Christmas and birthday celebrations, is always among the first to start work. On 12 January 1983 she was first off the mark with a visit to RAF Benson where the officers of the Queen's Flight are stationed. After posing for photographs with the officers and carrying out a formal inspection the Princess was entertained to lunch in the Officers' Mess. During lunch the Salon Orchestra of the Central Band of the RAF played to entertain her.

For the visit the Princess wore a stunning outfit entirely in keeping with the seasonal cold weather. The coat is of Persian lamb opulently trimmed at the neck, cuffs and hem with blue fox. The hat is made to match. It is a perfect outfit for keeping out the cold while simultaneously creating a sensation. Dressed like this the Princess looks more as though she has stepped out of a sleigh than a limousine.

On very formal evening occasions Princesses can create an impression with dresses which are as elaborate and eye catching as anything worn by their ancestors. They can also increase the 'royal' look by wearing a tiara, although this is done much less frequently than in the past. However, now that women's clothes are so much more casual and comfortable, the problem is to look fashionable during the day without disappointing the crowds, who expect royalty to look rather special. Princess Alexandra's particular success in projecting the right image, whatever the occasion, probably stems from the influence of her mother, Princess Marina, who was one of the most fashionable women of her generation. Princess Alexandra, like her mother, has always favoured styles which are elegant rather than gimmicky. Among her favourite designers are Donald Campbell and the Bellville Sassoon partnership. Day or evening, winter or summer, people are always delighted by Princess Alexandra's presence and style.

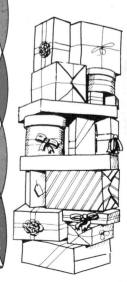

Diana's winter wardrobe

One of the aspects of the Christmas holiday the Princess of Wales enjoys most is the chance to be herself in the type of clothes she feels most comfortable in – casual separates, many of them from up-market chain stores like Benetton and Fiorucci. These are the sort of clothes she wore before her marriage and which she is still occasionally pictured in at informal occasions such as polo matches at Windsor. However, she knows that people would be disappointed to see her dressed like that all the time and has thrown herself whole-heartedly into acquiring a wardrobe which projects an image suitable for a future Queen. Most successful have been the dazzling ball gowns she has bought from designers like Emanuel, Gina Fratini and Bruce Oldfield. They make her look like a truly fairy-tale Princess. By wearing special dresses like these the Princess is paying a compliment to whoever is entertaining her and makes them feel they are indeed in the presence of someone very special.

The 'fairy-tale' quality of the Princess's evening wear is a feature which appeals to something in the Princess's nature for she often seems to favour the same approach in formal day clothes. One example was the dark green velvet suit with full skirt and leg-of-mutton sleeves which she wore during her first solo visit abroad – to Oslo in Norway. The suit looked almost as if it could have been worn by a daughter of Queen Victoria, although the effect was offset by the Princess's stylish modern hairstyle.

The same impression of a theatrical costume is conveyed by this cossack style coat worn on a visit to Gloucester Cathedral just before Christmas 1981. The coat, designed by Belville Sassoon, is made of grey flannel, trimmed with astrakhan and the Russian effect is emphasised by the frog-fastening at the front. The matching hat and muff are also of astrakhan. So great is the Princess's fashion influence that muffs instantly became a short-lived fashion success and sold out all over the country. No doubt many Christmas stockings had muffs in them that year.

A country girl at heart

Out walking at Sandringham the Duchess of Kent solved the problem of staying in style while keeping out the cold with this singularly appropriate sweater, showing a pipe-smoking snowman against a midnight blue background. Although she is over fifty, the Duchess has a remarkably youthful appearance which is partly due to her young style of dressing. She manages to catch the fashion mood with clothes like this trendy jumper but always looks dignified and elegant.

The Duke and Duchess used to live at Coppins, near Iver in Buckinghamshire, where the Duke was brought up with his sister, Princess Alexandra and brother Prince Michael. Unfortunately the charms of Coppins were severely threatened by its proximity to two motorways and in 1970 the Duke reluctantly decided to sell it. In 1973 the Kents moved to Anmer Hall which was given to them by the Queen. This late-Georgian house has four main bedrooms plus a nursery wing and staff quarters. It is in the village of Anmer which since the end of the nineteenth century has formed part of the Sandringham estate. One of the attractions of Anmer Hall is its closeness to the main house at Sandringham, but it also enjoys a great deal of privacy as it is set in ten acres of its own. While in London the Duke and Duchess live at York House, St James's Palace but they both enjoy getting away to the country. The Duchess, brought up in Yorkshire and educated at a school in Norfolk, is very much a country girl. However she is less keen on horsey pursuits than many of her relations and prefers to enjoy the country by striding out on foot. Her main talent is music – she studied music at Oxford, and she, like Princess Margaret, is often called upon to play carols and songs over Christmas. As part of their New Year holiday the Duke and Duchess of Kent also like to take their family away skiing. They are both keen skiers and so are their children, The Earl of St Andrews, Lady Helen Windsor and Lord Nicholas Windsor.

The Princesses' concern for children

Just before leaving Sandringham in February 1985 the Princess of Wales braved a heavy snowstorm to bring comfort to mothers assembled at Peterhouse, Cambridge, where scientists are investigating possible causes of infant deaths. The Princess is well known for her love of children. 'She loves young people and they adore her', says her father, Earl Spencer. Before her marriage she worked in a kindergarten and she is already the mother of two small sons of her own so she feels a special bond with other mothers and has a great compassion for those whose children have not been as fortunate as her own. She is always quick to bend down to the level of a child in a wheelchair or hospital bed and does not stand on ceremony when children try to touch her or hold her hand. Princess Anne has worked remarkably hard for the Save the Children Fund, much of whose work is done abroad. The Princess of Wales has so far concentrated her attention on children at home. This is reflected in some of the organisations of which she is Patron or President. These include the Malcolm

Sargent Cancer Fund for Children, Birthright, the Pre-School Playgroups Association, the three-year National Rubella Campaign, which aims to make everyone aware of the importance of being vaccinated against German Measles, and Dr Barnardo's, which she took over from Princess Margaret in 1985. One of her first functions as President of Dr Barnardo's was the typical combination of glamour and good works at which she excels. This was a charity fashion show held at a large London hotel by Bruce Oldfield, one of the Princess's favourite young designers and himself an 'old boy' of Dr Barnardo's. For the occasion the Princess wore a long pleated silver dress designed by Oldfield. Among those introduced to her was actress Joan Collins, also in an Oldfield dress. The Princess, who was not accompanied by Prince Charles, enjoyed herself tremendously and stayed dancing until well past midnight with, among others, actor Christopher Reeve and French composer Jean Michel Jarre. Her pleasure was all the greater because the evening raised a large sum of money for her charity.

Twelfth Night festivities

The old name for 6 January is Twelfth Night. It is the day for removing all signs of Christmas festivities until the following year, for according to tradition not to do so will bring bad luck. Since Twelfth Night occurs little more than a week after the royal party have arrived at Sandringham and put out all the cards and decorations they have brought with them from Windsor they do not take the warning very seriously and are inclined to leave the Christmas decorations on show right until the end of their holiday.

In recent years Twelfth Night has lost its importance as a Christmas festival, probably because we now enjoy so many more holidays than in past centuries, when Christmas was the main holiday of the year for most people. Then it was the custom for everyone to have one last party before returning to the serious business of life. This painting entitled 'Twelfth Night Feast' is by a Dutch artist, Jan Steen, and is in the Royal Collection. It shows an ordinary family enjoying themselves with plenty of food and party games for children and adults.

For hundreds of years Twelfth Night was marked by a riotous party at Court. A Lord of Misrule was appointed – the title went to whoever found a bean in the special Twelfth Night cake – and for the rest of the night he and his chosen lady ruled supreme, even over the King himself, with often outrageous results.

An Italian at the Court of Elizabeth I in 1600 describes elaborate Twelfth Night festivities which did not end until gone 2am. He describes the hall where the Queen dined as 'hanged with tapestries of gold' and the drinking vessels as covered with gold and jewels. 'Her Majesty mounted the stairs amid such sounding of trumpets that me thought I was on the field of war . . . As soon as her Majesty was set in her place many ladies and knights began a grand ball.' Shakespeare's play 'Twelfth Night', written especially for Elizabeth I, was performed for the first time on this occasion.

Feast of the Epiphany

The name given by the Church to Twelfth Night is the Feast of the Epiphany. It marks the end of the journey of the Three Wise Men who had followed the star to the birthplace of Jesus in Bethlehem. St Matthew describes the event in his Gospel:

> and, lo, the star, which they saw in the east, went before them, till it came and stood over where the young child was.
>
> When they saw the star, they rejoiced with exceeding great joy.
>
> And when they were come into the house, they saw the young child with Mary his mother, and fell down, and worshipped him: and when they had opened their treasures, they presented unto him gifts; gold, and frankincense, and myrrh.

On the Feast of the Epiphany a special service takes place in the Chapel Royal at St James's Palace at which the Sovereign offers gifts of gold, frankincense and myrrh to mark the fact that the Three Wise Men were also kings. Taking place where it does, it is a reminder that for several hundred years the Royal Christmas was spent at St James's Palace. There is a long tradition of gifts being offered by the Sovereign to the Church and the poor. It dates back to the time of William the Conqueror who presented gifts at Gloucester Cathedral when he wore his crown there at Christmas. The Tudors, like Elizabeth, and the Stuarts, such as Charles II, all made their offerings personally, but the custom changed with George III who preferred to leave it to his Lord Chamberlain. The Queen allows her gifts to be made by two of her Gentlemen Ushers. The 25 gold sovereigns she gives are converted to £25 for charity, the frankincense is given to an Anglican church to be used as incense and the myrrh is sent to Nashdom Abbey to make incense.

Music is provided by the Children and Gentlemen of the Chapel Royal who posed for this picture in one of the Palace courtyards. The Epiphany Service is open to the public and admission is by ticket applied for in advance.

The dashing Duke of Kent

Like his wife and children the Duke of Kent loves winter sports and greatly enjoys the annual family skiing holiday. The Duke was lucky enough to attend Le Rosey School in Switzerland where he took the opportunity to become highly proficient at the sport. While serving with the Royal Scots Greys he captained his regimental ski team in the 1961 Army Championships (the Duchess of Kent Cup). When he was younger the Duke preferred the faster events, the downhill and the slalom, and always managed to finish creditably in the front of the field.

Taking part in competitive skiing requires great nerve and in his quiet and understated way the Duke is surprisingly adventurous. He prefers to let the spotlight fall on his wife when they undertake public engagements, for example when as President of the All England Lawn Tennis Club he presents the trophies at Wimbledon. Yet he fully shares the Royal Family's sporting instincts and like his cousins is an accomplished horseman. He also holds a pilot's licence.

The photograph on the right was taken in winter 1965. It shows the Duke of Kent, totally unrecognisable and rather menacing in his protective helmet, goggles and suit, on the notorious Cresta Run at St Moritz in Switzerland. This icy helter-skelter for a one-man toboggan dates from 1884, and from 1892 in its present form. It is just over twelve hundred hair-raising metres long and once the toboggan leaves the top it can reach speeds of up to 85mph. The rider has only a small brake and his weight with which to control his speed and direction. Protective clothing is vital to cut down on the terrible bruises which even the most skilled tobogganist sustains if he brushes momentarily against the ice walls. Those who, like the Duke, have braved the Run and lived to tell the tale are automatically members of an élite club, many of whom gathered at St Moritz in 1984 to celebrate the Cresta Run's centenary.

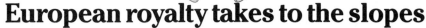

European royalty takes to the slopes

Early in 1985 Princess Caroline of Monaco enjoyed a skiing holiday at Gstaad in Switzerland with her husband, Italian Stefano Casiraghi, and her eight-month-old son Andrea (Andrew). The Princess is a devoted mother and took Andrea out on the slopes with her, carrying him, papoose style, on her back. On one day he even appeared wearing miniature sunglasses which exactly matched his mother's. You need to be a very confident skiier to go even a little way with a baby on your back, but Princess Caroline learned to ski almost as soon as she could walk, although she was not introduced to the sport quite as soon as Andrea. Monaco is ideally situated for anyone who, like the Princess, enjoys all sorts of sports and outdoor activities, winter or summer. Not only is it on the warm Mediterranean coast but the Alps are only a short drive away and it is possible to go skiing for a day or a weekend.

Princess Caroline's family, the Grimaldis, are not related to the British Royal Family in any way. However at Christmas the snow and the mountains exert a strong pull on many of the Queen's European relatives who get away if they can for a Christmas skiing holiday. King Juan Carlos of Spain and his wife Queen Sophia, who are both descended from Queen Victoria, usually take their three children to ski in the Pyrenees on the Eastern border of Spain, where they are sometimes joined by Queen Sophia's brother, ex-King Constantine of Greece, and his family. Crown Prince Harald of Norway and King Carl XVI Gustaf of Sweden, descendants of Queen Victoria, are also able to take their families skiing in their own countries. King Carl has a chalet at the Swedish resort of Storlein but he and Queen Silvia also try to take a skiing holiday in Gstaad where they meet up with many of their friends. The Dutch Royal Family can generally be found at the Austrian resort of Lech. For the royal families of Europe Christmas would not be Christmas without a skiing holiday.

Daring Prince Michael

Like so many of their relatives Prince and Princess Michael of Kent like to take winter sports holiday in the New Year. They are both excellent skiiers and enjoy going out on the slopes together. However, in the past Prince Michael has been extremely successful at another sport, bobsleighing. This is not dissimilar to the tobogganing enjoyed by his brother the Duke of Kent on the Cresta Run. Bobsleighing and tobogganing go back nearly nine thousand years, the oldest toboggan ever found was in Finland and dates from approximately 6500 BC. The first bobsleigh club was founded in 1887 at St Moritz, the home of the Cresta Run, and bobsleighing was included in the first winter Olympics at Chamonix in 1924. It is an extremely hard, fast and precarious sport, requiring split-second timing and nerves of steel both on the original four-man bobs and on the two-man boblets which hurtle down the mountain side at an even greater speed.

Prince Michael learned to bobsleigh at St Moritz in 1964 while he was with the army. He was a Regular Army Officer for nearly twenty years, serving first with the 11th Hussars (Prince Albert's Own) and later with the Defence Intelligence Staff. He finally left the army in 1981.

In 1966 Prince Michael began driving a two-man bob and was the fastest driver in the Inter-Services Bobsleigh Championships held at St Moritz in the same year and won by the army. In 1971 he took part in pre-Olympic trials in Japan and in January of that year represented Britain at the World Championships at Cervinia in Italy. In this photograph he can be seen in action with his brakeman, Michael Sweet. Unfortunately the pair experienced one or two hitches and came in 19th. In 1972 Prince Michael won the British Bobsleigh Championship at St Moritz and drove the British boblet in the European Championships, finishing 11th. In 1974 he retired from competitive driving but finds plenty of outlets for his energies and sense of adventure in hobbies which include flying, ballooning, deep-sea diving and carriage-driving.

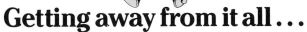

Getting away from it all...

Prince Charles first learned to ski at school in Gordonstoun, Scotland. He started to become a serious skiier in 1978 when he joined the Duke and Duchess of Gloucester for a holiday at the Swiss resort of Klosters and for the next few years a holiday at Klosters became a regular part of his winter break. As with every other challenging sport, once he had made up his mind to master skiing Prince Charles drove himself to the limits in order to achieve a really high standard and received some highly publicised falls along the way. The Princess of Wales also learned to ski while still at school and she is delighted to find one sport where she and the Prince are on equal terms.

The first skiing holiday they took together was marred for them by excessive press attention which the Princess clearly found rather upsetting. It is not possible to make skiing a private occupation – the hundreds of fellow skiiers would not take kindly to being turned off the mountain while the royal party skiied in peace. The Prince and Princess have therefore adapted their holiday to make the best possible compromise. For the last two years instead of going to Switzerland they have stayed at Vaduz Castle in the tiny principality of Liechtenstein, on the border between Austria and Switzerland. This has ensured they have somewhere truly private to escape to at the end of the day. The other response has been to develop a new 'tradition'. Before their holiday starts there is an official photo session at which the couple co-operate fully with photographers on the understanding they will be left in peace for the remainder of their stay. This proved a great success in 1984 and again in 1985 when they spent a five-day holiday at Maldun in Liechtenstein where a fresh fall of snow plus sunny weather created ideal skiing conditions. This photograph shows the Prince and Princess of Wales with their hosts Prince Hans-Adam of Liechtenstein and his wife, Princess Marie.

Princess Anne takes a break

Princess Anne and her husband Captain Mark Phillips are seen here enjoying a sledge made for two during a visit to Government House, Ottawa. This happy photograph was taken in New Year 1974, shortly after their marriage, when the couple paid an official visit to the Canadian capital. It was Captain Phillips's first experience of accompanying his wife in an official capacity. In succeeding years he has preferred to let her carry out most official engagements on her own. Now that he has left the army and farms their Gloucestershire estate, Gatcombe Park, he does not have time to be away. The Princess has increased her workload considerably since the early years when she was always falling foul of the press and is now one of the most admired members of the Royal Family. She never shirks any duty and has made many trips to visit troops in Germany and Northern Ireland. Much of her work is in connection with the Save the Children Fund of which she is President. She knows that her presence ensures that areas which badly need assistance will receive the publicity they deserve and so she makes many trips abroad on behalf of the Fund. In recent years she has visited Nepal, Swaziland, Zimbabwe, Malawi, Kenya, Somalia, Djibouti, North Yemen, Lebanon, Pakistan, The Gambia and Upper Volta. It would be impossible for her husband to spend so much time away from his own work. However their shared love of horses means they spend a lot of time together when the Princess is at home. Both are Olympic-class riders and since 1983 have organised One-Day Horse Trials at their home. The Princess is frequently photographed in headscarf and wellingtons helping to muck out the stables and set up the course. Because so much of her time is spent globe-trotting and performing public engagements the Princess welcomes Christmas as a time to relax with her family at Windsor and Sandringham. When the rest of the party starts to take off for the mountains of Europe she and Captain Phillips prefer to return to their horses at Gatcombe.

George V's imperial Christmas

Christmas in India is an exciting experience even for a King and the more so at the beginning of the century when travel was slower and more uncertain than it is today. In December 1911 George V became the first reigning British monarch to visit India. The November following his coronation in Westminster Abbey the King and Queen Mary set out for India by sea, arriving a month later. The main purpose of the visit was for the King to receive the homage of his Indian subjects as Emperor of India. This was done at the Great Durbar held at Delhi on 12 December. Durbar is an Indian word meaning a Court or audience and is best understood by looking at this painting, done by the official artist for the Indian journey, Jacomb Hood. The King and Queen had earlier ridden through the streets of Delhi to show themselves to their people. At the Durbar they received the homage of the native Indian rulers, the Maharajahs and Princes. George V and Queen Mary are depicted dressed magnificently in all their coronation robes and regalia, despite the intense heat, for the Durbar was in effect an important public relations exercise designed to display the magnificence of the King Emperor and it was vital that the royal pair were not outshone by the rich dress and jewellery of their subjects. George V was already showing he understood the importance of publicity, as he was to do later when he began the Christmas radio broadcasts. For the Indian tour he took both a photographer and a cameraman to take moving pictures. The film of the occasion, which was shown in cinemas throughout the country when the King and Queen returned to Britain, still exists today.

After the Durbar the King moved from the Imperial camp to Nepal in the foothills of the Himalayas. There the King and Queen Mary enjoyed a ten-day Christmas holiday, most of which was taken up by shooting tigers. It was in every way a far cry from Christmas at Sandringham and the pheasant shooting of previous years.

Acknowledgements

I should like to thank the many individuals and organisations who have helped me with this book, and the following in particular:

Miss Henrietta McBurney, Deputy Curator of the Print Room, Royal Library, Windsor Castle.

Marcus Bishop, Esq., The Lord Chamberlain's Office

Mrs Julia Harland, Assistant to The Surveyor of The Queen's Works of Art.

Miss Frances Dimond, Curator of the Photograph Collection, Royal Archives, Windsor Castle.

Sir Oliver Millar, The Surveyor of The Queen's Paintings.

Miss Theresa-Mary Morton, Photographic Department, Royal Library, Windsor Castle.

Major General R.L.C. Dixon, CB, MC, Chapter Clerk, St George's Chapel, Windsor.

Julian Lloyd, Esq., CVO and R.L. French, Esq., Estate Office, Sandringham.

Canon Caesar, Sub-Dean, Chapel Royal, St James's Palace.

The Press Office, Buckingham Palace.

The Office of HRH Princess Alice, Duchess of Gloucester.

The Office of Their Royal Highnesses the Duke and Duchess of Kent.

The Office of Their Royal Highnesses Prince and Princess Michael of Kent.

Oliver Davies, Esq., Keeper of Portraits, Royal College of Music.

Jane and Guy Woolfenden.

The British Limbless Ex-Service Men's Association.

The 'Not Forgotten' Association.

John Dinkel, Keeper of the Royal Pavilion, Brighton.

My assistant Jacqueline Bayes.